W9-BQX-703

THE WEST INDIES   Political Map

Names of cities over 1,000,000 are capitalized
National capitals   Santo Domingo
Secondary capitals   Bridgetown
——— ·—· Political Boundaries   ∿∿ Railroads

0   50   100   200 Miles
0   100   200   300 Kilometers

70°   65°   25°

A T L A N T I C

Tropic of Cancer

60°   55°

O C E A N

I   N   D   I   E   S

20°

Puerto Plata
Santiago   San Francisco
Mota del Macoris   CAPE SAMANÁ
10.417 La Vega   Sánchez   Samaná Bay
ICAN REPUBLIC
Santo
Domingo   San Pedro   Arecibo San Juan
Baní   de Macoris   Aguadilla   Caguas
CENTRAL   La Romana   Mayagüez   Charlotte Amalie
San Cristóbal   Mona   PUERTO RICO   VIRGIN IS.
Passage   Ponce   Guayama   ST CROIX
MONA   (U.S.A.)   (U.S.)
(P.R.)   Christiansted

C. ENGAÑO

ANEGADA
(Br.)
TORTOLA VIRGIN GORDA (Br.)
(Br.)
ST. JOHN (U.S.)   ANGUILLA
C. ST.   (Br.)
THOMAS   ST. MARTIN
(U.S.)   (Fr.-Neth.)
ST-BARTHÉLEMY (Fr.)   BARBUDA
(Br.)
SABA
(Neth.)   ST. KITTS
(Br.)
Basseterre   NEVIS   ANTIGUA
Charlestown   St. John's
MONTSERRAT   (Br.)
(Br.)

IOLA

L   E   S

Anegada Passage

Guadeloupe Passage
GUADELOUPE (Fr.)
DÉSIRADE (Fr.)
Soufrière
4869
Basse-Terre   Pointe-à-Pitre
LES SAINTES   MARIE GALANTE
(Fr.) Grand-Bourg   (Fr.)
Portsmouth   DOMINICA
(Br.)
Roseau

15°

Martinique Passage
Mt. Pelée
St-Pierre   MARTINIQUE
Fort-de-France   (Fr.)

S   E   A

St. Lucia Channel
Castries
ST. LUCIA
Soufrière   (Br.)

St. Vincent Passage
ST. VINCENT   BARBADOS
(Br.)   (Br.)
Kingstown   Bridgetown

WINDWARD   ANTILLES   IS.

L   E   S   S   E   R

ARUBA
(Neth.)
CURAÇAO
(Neth.)   BONAIRE
C. SAN ROMAN   (Neth.)   LOS ROQUES
PARAGUANÁ   (Ven.)   BLANQUILLA
PEN   Willemstad   AVES   ORCHILA   (Ven.)
(BIRD)   (Ven.)
(Ven.)
Venezuela   Coro

GRENADINES (Br.)
GRENADA
(Br.)
St. George's

TOBAGO

TRINIDAD
AND
TOBAGO

mas
unillas   Puerto Cabello   La Guaira   TORTUGA   MARGARITA
San Felipe   (Ven.)   (Ven.)   Carúpano
Barquisimeto   Valencia   Maracay   Cumana   Port of Spain   Arima
Puerto la Cruz   San Fernando   TRINIDAD
Barcelona   Maturín

V E N E Z U E L A

CARACAS

70°   65°   60°   10°

LIFE WORLD LIBRARY

THE WEST INDIES

TIME LIFE BOOKS ®

LIFE WORLD LIBRARY
LIFE NATURE LIBRARY
LIFE SCIENCE LIBRARY
THE LIFE HISTORY OF THE UNITED STATES
GREAT AGES OF MAN
TIME-LIFE LIBRARY OF ART
TIME READING PROGRAM
INTERNATIONAL BOOK SOCIETY

Life Pictorial Atlas of the World
The Epic of Man
The Wonders of Life on Earth
The World We Live In
The World's Great Religions
The Life Book of Christmas
Life's Picture History of Western Man
The Life Treasury of American Folklore
America's Arts and Skills
300 Years of American Painting
The Second World War
Life's Picture History of World War II
Picture Cook Book
Life Guide to Paris

LIFE WORLD LIBRARY

THE WEST INDIES

by Carter Harman

and The Editors of LIFE

TIME INCORPORATED   NEW YORK

COVER: Haitian women wearing
bright bandannas and cotton dresses
attend a busy outdoor market,
some bringing baskets
of farm produce to sell or barter.

ABOUT THE WRITER

Carter Harman, author of the interpretive text for this volume in the LIFE World Library, is a man of varied talents. Holder of a degree in music from Princeton University, Mr. Harman joined the U.S. Army Air Corps in 1942, became a squadron commander in Burma and was awarded the Distinguished Flying Cross for making the first helicopter rescue in history, picking up downed fliers behind enemy lines. After the war he served as a reporter and music critic for *The New York Times*. He became music editor of TIME in 1952. While in that post he wrote a successful book, *A Popular History of Music,* and composed a number of children's songs as well as an opera. He resigned in 1956 to record Caribbean music for an independent recording company, an interest derived from one of his TIME stories. Since then he has lived in Puerto Rico and visited virtually every island in the Caribbean. At present, he is at work on a historical novel, *Puerto Rico.*

The West Indies © 1963, 1966 Time Inc. All rights reserved. Published simultaneously in Canada.
Library of Congress catalogue card number 63-19904.
School and library distribution by Silver Burdett Company.

Contents

TIME-LIFE BOOKS

EDITOR
Maitland A. Edey
TEXT DIRECTOR   ART DIRECTOR
Jerry Korn   Edward A. Hamilton
CHIEF OF RESEARCH
Beatrice T. Dobie
Assistant Text Director: Harold C. Field
Assistant Art Director: Arnold C. Holeywell
Assistant Chiefs of Research:
Monica O. Horne, Martha Turner

•

PUBLISHER
Rhett Austell
General Manager: Joseph C. Hazen Jr.
Business Manager: John D. McSweeney
Circulation Director: Joan D. Manley
Publishing Board: Nicholas Benton, Louis Bronzo.
James Wendell Forbes, John S. Wiseman

LIFE MAGAZINE

EDITOR: Edward K. Thompson
MANAGING EDITOR: George P. Hunt
PUBLISHER: Jerome S. Hardy

LIFE WORLD LIBRARY

SERIES EDITOR: Oliver E. Allen
Editorial Staff for *The West Indies:*
Assistant Editor: Jay Brennan
Designer: Ben Schultz
Chief Researcher: Grace Brynolson
Researchers: Paula von Haimberger Arno, Edward Brash,
Mary Elizabeth Davidson, Helen Harman, Madeleine Richards,
Helen R. Turvey, Linda Wolfe, Owen Fang

EDITORIAL PRODUCTION
Color Director: Robert L. Young
Copy Staff: Marian Gordon Goldman, Carol Henderson,
Dolores A. Littles
Picture Bureau: Margaret K. Goldsmith, Sue Bond
Art Assistants: James D. Smith, James K. Davis

The text for this book was written by Carter Harman, the picture essays by David S. Thomson and Sam Halper. The following individuals and departments of Time Inc. were helpful in producing the book: Leonard McCombe and Grey Villet, LIFE staff photographers; Doris O'Neil, Chief of the LIFE Picture Library; Richard M. Clurman, Chief of the TIME-LIFE News Service; and Peter Draz, Chief of the Bureau of Editorial Reference.

Introduction

The West Indies, next after the East Indies, is the most strategically placed, overpopulated, ethnologically complex and politically divided archipelago on earth. Aside from a few vacation spots, the American public knows little of it. Historically, the dominant power in the Caribbean Sea has been the dominant power in the Western Hemisphere. The islands of the Greater and Lesser Antilles, a great crescent reaching from Florida to the South American shoulder, have been and still are the classic keys to Caribbean penetration.

No picture of the whole region and its salient characteristics, colors and conflicts had been presented (so far as I know) until the trail-breaking job here offered by Mr. Carter Harman. Neither he nor anyone could exhaust the area's combined romance, beauty, danger and passion, or do justice to its combined possibilities, capacities, achievements and hopes. Few analysts would agree with all of any single account: the problems are too complex, deep and varied. West Indian history began more than 100 years before the continental United States was settled at all. Plunder, product and trade arising from the region's development revolutionized European economic life and its monetary as well as maritime evolution. As a unit, the archipelago might have been a powerful independent force; conquests, diplomatic bickerings, European power politics, piracy and the slave trade instead left it a patchwork of separate nations, languages, races and cultures.

Clearly the area can have a brilliant future.

The renascence of Puerto Rico—the best single job of rapid political, social and economic construction in the world—demonstrates that fact. If this book does no more than indicate the richness as well as the problems of the region, its purpose will have been served. One need not take as complete its account of the turmoil in the Dominican Republic; one may differ with its emphasis on the *vodou* rites in Haiti. Yet the fact is that no single author, aside from Mr. Harman, has attempted to present a whole picture of this intricate chain of islands.

For they are now interconnected in their own right and on their own ground. This is new. When I was young, one could travel from San Juan, Puerto Rico, to Port-au-Prince, Haiti, only by steaming to New York and coming back. Since World War II most if not all major islands have been linked to each other by air; their radios talk to each other continuously; they impact upon each other and upon the Caribbean littoral. It remains to be seen whether the archipelago will become anew the cockpit of world politics, as it was during the naval and revolutionary struggles of European nations during the 17th and 18th Centuries. In the New World, the region is now a top problem: war and peace may well depend on the outcome of its affairs. Latin American nations on the continent can base their lives on their own internal structures. The West Indies, fatefully lying across major trade routes, must depend for their peace in large measure on better organization of the affairs of the world. It is time for Americans to know them well.

ADOLF A. BERLE
*former Assistant Secretary of State
for Latin American Affairs*

1

A Paradise in Ferment

AN American astronaut making his re-entry into the atmosphere downrange from Cape Kennedy would, if he had a chance to look out, see the entire oval shape of the Caribbean Sea. It would glow a luminous blue, gilded here and there with sunlight. To the west and south, the Central American isthmus and the northern shore of South America—once called the "Spanish Main"—would limit the sea's expanse; three big islands jutting out from the tip of Florida would limit it on the north. A gentle crescent of smaller islands would barricade the sea on the east. This is the warm, seemingly languorous, wind-washed region that Columbus likened to a paradise, the West Indies where world powers once believed they could find the key to the future, where over the centuries the proportion of anguish per square mile has been perhaps higher than anywhere on earth, and where visions of immeasurable wealth often blew away in the violent wind.

The island chain looks like a long skeletal tail whipping out from the largest island, Cuba. The easterly shore of each island is whitened by the frosting of wind-driven Atlantic rollers. Tucked safely in a leeward bay, there is usually the nugget of a city. Among the cumulus clouds, occasional towering thunderheads seem to stand on thick, gray, hazy columns—the drenching showers that keep the islands fertile. On every side are vivid colors, from the rich blues of sea and sky to the fiery punctuation of tropical blossoms on a dozen shades of luxuriant green. In the distance is the jagged shape of mountains, their peaks and ridges capped with clouds.

The islands are a densely populated paradise. In a total land area of 91,000 square miles, there are an estimated 19 million inhabitants. Every hillside is thickly salted with thatched or tin-roofed shacks and the coastal cities are cuddled by sprawling shantytowns. In the busy cities, sidewalks bustle with pedestrians. Barefooted grandmothers in old-fashioned full skirts and bandannas contrast with swaying high-heeled girls in tight dresses; plump, dark-skinned businessmen in white duck and gold-rimmed spectacles jostle with dusty pushcart vendors and country people carrying bundles of produce on their heads. Adding to the impression of denseness are the pungent odors that thicken the atmosphere: the unforgettable smells of burning charcoal, coconut husks and hot fat. The air rings with street vendors' cries, the semimusical thunking of a steel band tuning up in somebody's back yard, the shrill voices of gossiping women, and the impatient clatter and beep of the latest traffic jam.

These 7,000-odd islands and reefs were the outposts of the New World, whose written history began with a jolt one October day in 1492 when Christopher Columbus waded ashore on what was probably San Salvador in the Bahamas, convinced that he had reached the back door of India. When he called the islands the Indies, he set in motion a pattern of misunder-

NAMES FROM THE DAYS OF SAIL

The division of the eastern crescent of the West Indies into the Windward and Leeward Islands dates back to the days of sail, but the designations are confusing. To sailors, "windward" means the direction from which the wind is coming, "leeward" the direction toward which it is blowing. The trade wind blows over the West Indies from an easterly direction. The northern British islands were originally named the Leewards because they lay to leeward of the important colony of Barbados. The southern group, which lies to windward of the Spanish-held mainland, was for that reason named the Windwards. The entire eastern group is also known as the Lesser Antilles, the Greater Antilles being the islands west of the British and U.S. Virgins. The word "Antilles" derives from "Antillia," a legendary island which some of Columbus' contemporaries thought he had reached.

standing which still continues, and which is aggravated by a welter of historical confusion.

Almost from the beginning, all of the islands, including the larger ones of Cuba, Hispaniola and Puerto Rico, were called the West Indies, although much of the English-speaking world, in the course of time, came to apply the term only to the British West Indies. The olive-skinned peoples who lived on the islands before Columbus' arrival—the Arawak, Carib and Ciboney—naturally had to be called Indians. The people who live there now are called West Indians, no matter what their races or colors; among them are perhaps 300,000 so-called East Indians who are not, however, from the East Indies but from India. On maps, the West Indies are also named the Antilles; in the past the islands were also often called the Caribbees.

Although the brawling adventurers who followed Columbus brought their pickaxes to dig for gold, the first real importance of the West Indies was quasi-military; the best harbors were fortified to provide refuge for Spanish galleons homeward bound with treasures from the great troves the conquistadors discovered and looted in Mexico and Peru, while the smaller coves and inlets became nests for the swift-moving raiders that darted out to prey on them. The great turning point in modern West Indies history was also military in origin. Population movements begun in World War I, and accelerated in World War II, awakened the islanders to the fact that there was a world outside, a world where a laborer might rise to the level of a landowner or at the very least might have a hand in shaping his own future.

Between these two significant moments in time, Europeans discovered that the islands could be turned to profit despite their lack of gold. The soil was remarkably fertile, and at first there seemed to be a supply of native labor; the Europeans turned to the cultivation of sugar cane, and when the cane flourished, the Western world found its first adequate supply of sweetening—and concomitantly became entangled in the monstrous exploitation of African slaves.

For close to four centuries the West Indies existed without creating any history of their own; each island oriented itself toward its distant mother country in Europe and stubbornly ignored its Caribbean neighbors—despite the fact that the neighbors were frequently visible on the horizon. Then, starting after the emancipation of the slaves in the 19th Century, there began an awakening —slow, uncertain, interrupted by episodes of appalling savagery, but nevertheless an awakening. That phenomenon, however, was not to become noticeable for almost two generations.

From time immemorial, the most important physical element contributing to the nature and development of the West Indian islands has been the trade wind. It blows more or less steadily from an easterly direction throughout most of the year, moving at a rather brisk pace on the surface and considerably faster at the altitude of 2,500 feet. The islands lie directly in its path. Through the centuries the trade wind helped unguessed numbers of seeds and spores to drift across the Atlantic Ocean, probably including the seed pods of the ubiquitous coconut. The trade wind also enabled men, from the earliest Spanish conquistadors to the thousands of slavers, to make voyages that would often have been impossible in less favorable latitudes.

CREOLE: WHAT THE WORD MEANS

The word "Creole" so often heard in the West Indies creates endless confusion, for it can be used to designate a language, a person, an entire society or even a style of cooking. When used for a person, it means someone of European ancestry—a child of Spanish parents, for example—who is born in the New World, and his descendants. Creole tongues are actual languages, not merely dialects; French Creole, for example, uses a vocabulary which is basically French but has a non-French grammatical system that may be African in origin. Originally, masters taught slaves a kind of baby-talk version of their own language ("Me want you go there"). This simple tongue was of course inadequate; to talk to each other and their children, the slaves gradually expanded it with additional words, gave it structure and thus eventually created a full-fledged language.

Without the wind, even if they had succeeded in crossing the Atlantic, the explorers probably would have found only barren and forbidding rock. Instead they discovered flora fighting for space to proliferate on sweeping flatlands. For the trade wind carries along the moisture that rises from the tossing sea and stores it in cumulus clouds; some of the clouds precipitate in the random showers that may be seen everywhere in the Caribbean. But when the breeze encounters the side of a mountain, the slopes divert it upward into the cooler altitudes. The cooling causes the moisture to condense and form drops of water. Rain clouds daily may be seen trailing from the mountain summits like smoke from factory chimneys, striping the countryside below with life-giving moisture. Between showers, the hot tropical sun adds its form of nourishment, helping to make abundant growth possible even in exhausted soil.

In the high rain forest areas more than 200 inches of rain precipitate annually. Over the centuries, incalculable tons of water rushing down the steep hillsides have washed away vast quantities of earth, depositing it in the plains and valleys below to form what is technically known as alluvial soil. In this soil, bananas, breadfruit, mangoes, cassava, coconuts, citrus fruits and a variety of edible roots grow in abundance. More important to the islands is the fact that this rich alluvial soil is equally suitable for the cultivation of the cash crops of sugar, tobacco, coffee, cocoa and spices.

The trade wind is also partly responsible for that less benign phenomenon of the Caribbean area, the late summer storm called hurricane. Most hurricanes are born slightly north of the equator, somewhere to the east of the

Caribbean Sea. These storms usually move into the Caribbean near Guadeloupe and St. Christopher (an island generally called St. Kitts) and then curve northward, providing an annual threat to them and to Antigua, Barbuda and the more westerly islands.

The blast of hurricane wind is like a giant fist which can flatten houses, people and fruit trees with equal ease. The destruction is completed by torrents of rain water which can flush whole plantations down a hillside, leaving a raw, red river bed where thousands of dollars' worth of coffee trees or tobacco plants or sugar cane had been growing the day before. Since people started keeping track of them, there has rarely been a year without one or more hurricanes in the Caribbean area. Not all of them touch land, however, and it is not uncommon for islands to go for 10 years without being struck. In the Virgin Islands, October 25 is declared a holiday and thanks are offered if there has been no hurricane damage that season. The southernmost islands are safer: Trinidad has not been hit since 1933.

A GLANCE at the map conveys the impression that the West Indian islands are a geographical unit, as if the jagged island shapes were really the peaks of submerged mountain ranges; and that is exactly what they are. Millennia ago, the basin now occupied by the Caribbean Sea may have stood so high that the islands constituted part of a continuous land mass, possibly connected to Florida. At some point the land sank into the sea like the legendary continent of Atlantis. Mountainsides of impassable steepness thrust high into the air during the course of the cataclysm, and giant sections split away to leave cliffs of terrifying grandeur standing in the sea. Meanwhile, other islands were formed as volcanoes thrust up through the waters.

The process of geological adjustment is of course never complete, and the West Indies remain subject to earthquakes that shake the susceptible islands like St. Thomas measurably and often perceptibly several times a week the year around. When the tremors are felt, people stop where they stand, spines tingling, feeling the movement beneath their feet, and knowing there is no place to go.

Whatever geologic heritage they may share, the Caribbean islands remain politically disparate. Their peoples have created three relatively mature nations—the Republic of Haiti, which obtained its independence in 1804, the Dominican Republic (1844) and Cuba (1902). Two new countries—Jamaica, and Trinidad and Tobago —were created in 1962, while Barbados and the mainland colony of British Guiana (Guyana) were scheduled for independence in 1966.

NOT quite independent, but operating with almost complete autonomy, are Puerto Rico, which achieved its U.S. "commonwealth" status in 1952, and the Netherlands Antilles, a largely self-governing part of the Kingdom of the Netherlands since 1954. The Netherlands Antilles are made up of the islands of Aruba, Bonaire, Curaçao, St. Eustatius (often called "Statia") and Saba, and part of the island of Sint Maarten. Martinique and Guadeloupe are overseas *départements* of France; Guadeloupe, in turn, has its own dependencies of Désirade, Les Saintes, Marie-Galante, Saint-Barthélemy and the rest of Sint Maarten, known to the French as Saint-Martin. The status of some 200 minor islands and cays, or reefs, and six principal islands of the British West Indies—Grenada, St. Vincent, St. Lucia, Dominica, St. Kitts and Montserrat—is unsettled. In 1966, Antigua planned to become an autonomous associated territory, related to England somewhat as Puerto Rico is to the U.S. The British Virgin Islands are a colony, as are the distant British Caymans. The 700 islands and more than 2,000 cays called the Bahamas retain, with few indications of political discontent, the ancient and nonautonomous status of a British colony. The United States Virgin Islands, St. Thomas, St. Croix and St. John, are U.S. possessions with limited self-government.

The disparity of life in these islands is underlined by a veritable babel of European and local languages: French and the French-derived Creole spoken in Martinique, Guadeloupe, Haiti and other islands formerly held by the French; the Spanish of Cuba, the Dominican Republic and Puerto Rico; the Dutch of the Netherlands Antilles; and the Spanish-Portuguese-English-Dutch language called Papiamento, which is used on Aruba, Bonaire and Curaçao. English is spoken on the Dutch islands as well as on the British and American ones, and it is widely understood elsewhere.

Further separation among the islands is encouraged by the use of ten currencies: U.S. dollars, East Caribbean dollars, Trinidad-Tobago dollars, Dominican pesos, Jamaican and British pounds, Cuban pesos, Haitian gourdes, Martiniquan francs and Netherlands Antilles guilders.

The divergences among the islands and their peoples are the result of processes set in motion long ago, in the 17th Century period when the European powers began to exploit the area in earnest. The Europeans operated the island plantations and their slave workers as commercial properties, using both to produce staples for the European markets. The colonists were rough men who "went out" to the tropics for a limited period to make their fortunes. They endured the heat, the disease, the remoteness and the mutinous slaves; most of them could not be bothered with anything so frivolous as social graces or intellectual pursuits or even with making the insides of their big houses comfortable. They made their money in the islands and spent it grandly in the cities of Europe, where "rich as a West Indies planter" became a common phrase.

ON many islands the plantations were from the beginning placed in the hands of hired managers. The result was a situation that virtually invited irresponsibility, for the managers had less interest in the property than the planters, no concern for the slaves and little supervision—except for a visit every few years from an owner.

To hold the vast numbers of slaves in line, the slaveowners kept them in ignorance—for education had already been recognized as a first step toward a desire for freedom. They also kept them disorganized and in terror of brutal punishment. But although most colonial planters regarded their slaves as little more than animals, they had no reluctance in taking the prettier girls as sexual partners and even as established concubines. Inevitably many of these men developed affection for their women and for their children and frequently gave them their freedom (sometimes this was immediate; sometimes manumission was withheld until the planter's death). As a result, another class, free people of mixed parentage, came into existence. The importance of these people to West Indian society is large. Both colonists and slaves often treated them as a separate, contemptible and threatening race; yet they multiplied until they heavily outnumbered the whites, and eventually many of them became educated and even propertied. In the English islands they were called "free colored" or simply "colored people." In the French islands they were known as *gens de couleur* or *affranchis* (freed ones); in the Spanish islands, where color has been of less importance, they were referred to as *libertos* or *emancipados*.

TODAY, the overwhelming majority of the population of the West Indies is dark-skinned. Proportions of whites run as low as a fraction of 1 per cent in such remote British islands as Barbuda; the average is about 2 per cent white in the British islands, somewhat higher in the French, and about 50 per cent in Puerto Rico and about 30 per cent in Cuba and the Dominican Republic where the sugar business, which brought the slaves, was late in developing. The exact proportion of persons of mixed ancestry is literally anybody's guess; European ancestry is, for obvious reasons in a onetime slave society, a desirable possession, even in small proportions, and is claimed whenever possible. Negro ancestry is sometimes denied when appearances permit.

The remains of the class distinctions of colonial days permeate the West Indies—although they are somewhat less clearly drawn along color lines in the Hispanic islands than in the others. The "lowest" class generally consists of rural laborers with dark skins and limited education. The next "higher" is made up of urban professionals of mixed European and African ancestry. Ordinarily the "highest" is formed of white landowners who, despite their tiny minority, still control most of the power in the islands.

THE rural worker often lives in a wattle-and-daub hut pegged to a hillside on stilts, without water or sanitation; he is the builder, planter and cane cutter while his woman is the cultivator of their garden and the toter of produce and water. The typical rural worker is poorer than an outsider can easily believe possible, having only a few cents a week to buy clothes for his family and whatever food he and his wife cannot grow. During the sugar growing and harvesting season, he may today collect the highest wages he ever earned, as much as $4.22 a day in Puerto Rico. He remains proud, dignified, stoic and occasionally sullen; but sometimes, even in the desperately poor Republic of Haiti, he is astonishingly ready to return a smile for a stranger's smile.

In the rural areas in the West Indies, a typical sight is a file of erect and dusty women on their way to market with baskets on their heads. A common sight in the cities is a group of trim office or sales girls, dressed in uniform dark skirts and white blouses. They use bright lipstick and earrings and favor the latest hairdos. They are poorly paid, and their work performance, by North American standards, is inefficient. They spend a considerable part of their income on appearance and, perhaps because of dietary deficiencies, their teeth are probably unhealthy—although less obviously so than a few years ago; the exclusive use of gold for caps and fillings is disappearing along with the steel-rimmed spectacles long favored by West Indian men. In the French and English islands, the working girls frequently show striking combinations of Oriental, Negroid and Caucasian characteristics. In the Hispanic islands antecedents are not so easily identifiable, but the *piel-de-canela* — cinnamon-colored skin — and the women's gait are distinctively Latin American.

The time-tattered description of the healthy West Indian is valid. His body is strong, lithe and straight, and it moves with a rhythm that is the joy and despair of urban white men; his children learn to dance as soon as they walk. His music is gentle, melodious and irrepressible; if, as in Trinidad, he is denied his drums, he develops a substitute—the steel band. He speaks with a dry and subtle wit that cheers his companions. His love life appears free and easy —the percentage of so-called legitimate births throughout the Caribbean area is still very low—but turns out to be not as free as it appears, because of rules imposed by his own society.

He thinks of himself as a human being among other human beings, and he knows he may ordinarily work and live wherever he wishes and marry whomever he pleases. This does not mean that he is not conscious of gradations in skin color. He may, for example, believe that he is marrying well if his bride is light-complexioned. A mother may favor a light-skinned child because she thinks it has a better chance in the world. Straight hair is known as "good" hair. A café-au-lait member of the bourgeoisie may express shock on discovering the eminence of a darker-skinned man. In some islands few white men would consider going into politics; almost certain failure would result. If a very light-skinned young person should reach a situation when he must decide whether to pass as white, he goes through agonies of soul-searching.

BUT this color consciousness seems little more serious than that of members of any competitive society trying to achieve the best possible lives for themselves and their children. Color prejudice in the Caribbean is gentle compared to what might be called the area's "culture prejudice." Education is the basic social standard; the most damning term a polite

West Indian can apply to another is "illiterate." Even far from home the West Indian maintains this feeling. A West Indian Negro in New York acts superior to local Negroes because he thinks they speak poorly.

Relatively few people of the West Indies were aware of the world outside their islands before World War II. Nor did they realize that some of the problems of their paradise might be cured or at least alleviated. Radio and motion pictures, which began to come within the reach of the poor, provided dreams of a better life, but the West Indians did not presume to take them seriously. However, the thousands of American servicemen stationed around the Caribbean and the demand for local labor to work on the new United States bases did provide unprecedented contact—one aspect of the experience was recorded in such rueful Calypso-style songs as *Rum and Coca-Cola* and *Brownskin Gal*—and the dreams began to seem somewhat less ephemeral.

The need for labor produced a movement of population from the fields to the cities. Inevitably, the pace of life was stepped up throughout the islands. The demand for education and technical training increased. The development of long-range passenger planes made legendary lands abroad into accessible neighbors. West Indian people for the first time began to hope for something better than their old lives. And they came to see value in their racial heritage. In the years since the end of the war, this has led to a restless and sometimes misdirected striving for the kind of attention the newly born nations in Africa were receiving.

ISLANDS SELDOM NOTICED

In addition to the islands of the West Indies which attract both tourist and international attention, the broad area of the Caribbean contains a vast number of islands and islets which seldom make even the travel pages. Largest of them is Margarita. Lying off the coast of Venezuela, it has been a profitable source of pearls for more than 400 years and has in recent years become a Venezuelan resort. Venezuela also owns nearby Aves (Bird) Island, whose sole inhabitants are the sea birds which give it its name; Aves is only a few feet above sea level. Off Nicaragua but owned by Colombia are Vieja Providencia and San Andrés. First occupied by the Dutch, and later seized by the English privateer Henry Morgan, they were at one time or another occupied by virtually every European power with a Caribbean interest. Nearby are Great Corn and Little Corn, on which the United States took a lease from Nicaragua shortly before World War I, when there was discussion of cutting an additional channel to the Pacific near the Panama Canal. Ownership of the Swan Islands which lie between Cuba and Honduras, and on which the U.S. maintains a radio-broadcasting and weather station, is disputed by the U.S. and Honduras.

Nevertheless innumerable problems have remained. Throughout the smaller islands, the changing economic realities of the 20th Century have been destroying markets abroad and causing the younger generation—the bulk of the labor force—to leave home and find work in other lands; even with extreme measures the outlook for these islands appears bleak. In the mid-1960s, there was continuing agitation in Martinique and Guadeloupe for the loosening of the close embrace that entwined them with France, and variants of the pattern were affecting the big islands to the north. Puerto Rico was still testing a novel and daring way out of the doldrums of colonyhood. Haiti was suffering under the latest incarnation in a series of unscrupulous political adventurers. The Dominican Republic was trying to create a decent social structure out of the ruins left by an assassinated dictator who had drained the country for a generation. In Cuba the once high-principled revolution had turned grim, casting the ominous shadow of Communism across the Western Hemisphere.

Over the centuries, the West Indies have seemed a paradise to some of the new arrivals—to the explorers who looked with awe on their fierce luxuriance, to the planters who reaped wealth from their fertile soil, to the city-weary tourists who became euphoric in their sun and wind. To the vast numbers of Africans who arrived in the packed hulls of the slavers, the lovely islands appeared not a paradise but a hell. In the 1960s, it became clear that the descendants of the Africans were actively trying to remodel paradise to suit their own needs.

HUSKING COCONUTS, two big, heavily muscled Trinidadians *(left)* dig out the meaty kernels with their knives. Dried, the meat is pressed to obtain coconut oil, used in making shortening and other products.

WAITING TO BARGAIN, women in bright dresses and kerchiefs *(opposite)* throng an open-air bazaar on the curving terraces of a Haitian hill town. The merchants display their goods in thatch-roofed booths.

A Vivid Mixing of Handsome and Vital Peoples

The densely populated islands of the West Indies form one of the most variegated areas on earth. A dozen ethnic strains have settled there, making the people a vibrant composite of Europe, Africa and the East. Combinations of these strains have produced inhabitants who for harmony and variety of hue and lineament are incomparable. The islands themselves, although washed by the same sea, also show considerable variety. Some still remain almost wholly agricultural while other islands have turned briskly to 20th Century trade and industry. Some have striven, bloodily or peacefully, for freedom while others have remained colonies. But whatever the state of their economies or governments, they each dazzle the visitor with their vivid natural beauty and with the ebullient, cheerful vitality of their people.

GAILY DRESSED GIRLS, one carrying her little brother, stride down a roadway overlooking the shanties of a slum district of Santiago, the second-largest city of the Dominican Republic. Few Dominican houses have running water and many, like these, are roofed with thatch or rags. As on numerous other islands, there is need here for extensive housing reforms.

NEIGHBORHOOD PUMP attracts a cluster of Haitians with a bizarre assortment of cans and buckets. This single pump supplies water for a large section of suburban Port-au-Prince.

OPEN-SIDED BUS called *L'Aurore (below)* is jammed with people as it makes its runs from Port-au-Prince to outlying districts. The passengers often sing in unison to beguile the trip.

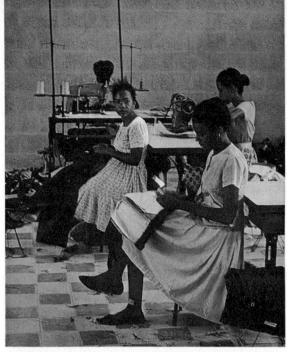

IN A TIDY SHOP run by an agency of the French government, four women of Martinique learn tailoring. The French have been active in setting up training programs on their islands.

IN A SMALL CHURCH on Jamaica, elderly Catholics, dressed in their Sunday best, file into their pews. Most Jamaicans are Protestant, but the Catholic Church has gained a foothold here.

IN A SUNNY SCHOOL in St.-Pierre, Martinique, adult students (left) take an examination in rock types. Trained by the government, they will become managers of rural cooperatives.

IN A FULL-DRESS PARADE, members of several Kingston, Jamaica, benevolent societies march beneath colorful banners accompanied by their scrubbed and spotless children. Kingston has a number of these societies which were originally formed to give dues-paying members fine, dignified funerals when they died. Today they also serve as centers of social activity.

HINDU GIRLS in Trinidad enjoy a school snack of crackers and milk. Some 134,000 people from India were recruited as laborers by Trinidad in the 19th Century, and their descendants make up more than 35 per cent of the island's population.

ONE-ROOM SCHOOLHOUSE on St. Christopher (usually referred to as St. Kitts) has space for several primary grades. A small British-owned island, St. Kitts has 18 government-supported primary schools but only three secondary schools.

2

The Race
for Riches

GEOLOGISTS divide the West Indian islands of the Caribbean into two major
ranges: one of Cuba, Jamaica, Hispaniola and
Puerto Rico thrusting out from Central America
and fragmenting in the Virgin Islands to the east,
the other an arc bending southward from St.
Croix toward Trinidad and containing all the
Windward and Leeward Islands. The Europeans
who settled the area are also divided into two
groups: the Spaniards, who were first on the
scene, and all the others. Between them the
invaders turned the placid Caribbean Sea into
a cockpit of turmoil, virtually snuffing out
one entire race—the so-called Indians who had

inhabited the area—and so completely domi-
nating the Negroes they brought from Africa
that, although the darker-skinned people outnumbered the whites from the beginning, their
voices were not to be heard in the administration of the region for centuries.

It was an unlovely mob that spread itself
over the New World. Its leaders were driven by
a consuming greed that outweighed honor and
humanity. In some cases they turned into true
heroes, in others into monsters. The mob's
second rank consisted of roughnecks and op-
portunists who were sent out to consolidate
the gains of the first group. They too were

motivated by avarice; but for occasional flashes of heroism, they substituted treachery, jealousy, slander, double-dealing and irascibility. There were of course some genuine idealists and malcontents whose religious or political beliefs had made their lives intolerable in the homeland, and there were many poor simply in search of land and a better life. But there were many more delinquents, rowdies, bad risks and jailbirds whose presence could no longer be tolerated on the muddy streets of Europe. Many of the women—among them trollops, pickpockets and harridans—who followed, sometimes in shipload lots, were their match in every way.

THE Europeans' early days in the New World were by no means easy. Columbus returned to Europe with only charts, promises and just enough gold to pique Queen Isabella's curiosity; he was allowed to sail again, but the story of his second, third and fourth voyages is a sorry tale of more and more desperate scrabbling for something concrete enough to restore his fortunes at court. On his last voyage, the queen's men would not even allow him to land in the new town of Santo Domingo, on the island he had himself discovered. The first British in Barbados spent so much time quarreling over boundaries and titles that they neglected their fields and came close to starvation. The first French in St. Kitts were so peeved at what they took to be their abandonment by the home office that they decided to give up the colony; in order to depart with something of value, they planted their entire acreage, so painfully cleared, in tobacco, digging up their food crops to do so. When they were rescued by a Dutch merchantman, they were starving.

Columbus had set out not to prove that the world was round—only diehard conservatives denied that fact—but to make use of the roundness to sneak in the back door of Marco Polo's fabled Asia. Columbus came close to disaster because he—like most navigators of his time—thought the globe was only one third of its actual size; his salvation lay in his remarkably fast crossing. He was fortunate on that first

voyage to escape hurricanes and to find wooded islands of surpassing beauty and fertility.

Among the immediate results of his voyage were the four famous Papal Bulls of Alexander VI, which in 1493 divided the lands beyond the horizon between Spain and Portugal. Spain was awarded all of its past discoveries and whatever future discoveries its captains might make beyond a pole-to-pole line 100 leagues west of the Azores (subsequently increased to 370 leagues). Since the line sliced through what is now Brazil, the eastern part of that land was handed to Portugal, along with all of Africa. The entire West Indies was Spain's bailiwick.

On his second voyage, in 1493, Columbus commanded a 17-ship, 1,200-man expedition that was thoughtfully equipped with tools, seeds and animals to establish a self-supporting base in Hispaniola. But though Columbus was a genius as a navigator, on shore he was something less, and he had difficulties with the hot-headed members of his expedition. Many of his workmen and farmers fell ill, and the gentlemen-adventurers who had accompanied the expedition were not at all interested in laborers' work. They had come to discover gold; the Indians could till the soil.

THE "Indians" discovered by Columbus were Arawaks. They looked, he wrote, rather like Canary Islanders, "neither black nor white." They were a gentle people occupied mostly in fishing and agriculture, and they were generous to arriving mariners. From the Arawaks, the Spaniards learned to make bread out of the poisonous cassava, or manioc, root, how to sleep in hammocks and how to smoke tobacco. In return the Spaniards offered death from smallpox, overwork and warfare. The Indians gave Columbus' men golden trinkets, but the Spaniards wanted more. They wanted laborers for the fields and mines, and they wanted women, too.

Soon the Spaniards began to move through the Caribbean like warrior ants, taking what they pleased, victimizing and often killing the natives. They spread eastward from Hispaniola only as far as Puerto Rico. In the easterly islands they encountered some Indians as murderous as themselves: the Caribs, a fierce, seagoing people from South America who liked to eat their enemies (*caríbal* is an obsolete variant of *caníbal*) and to paint themselves red. The conquistadors moved more swiftly westward, for in that direction lay the legendary city of gold called El Dorado and, past it, the untold wealth of Asia. By 1519 they were in Mexico and by 1522 in Peru, and by 1525 they stood on the northern coast of South America.

IT was more than a century after the Spanish discovery of the New World before any other power was able to establish a firm foothold in the Caribbean. Other European nations were engaged through the period of Spain's early conquests in the Americas in dynastic feuds, religious quarrels and warfare in the East with the expanding Turkish empire. Other countries were of course interested in the wealth of the New World, but for the most part their forays were carried out by private individuals or companies of traders and adventurers operating at their own risk. These expeditions took two forms, smuggling and freebooting.

The smuggling was inspired by the mercantilist policy pursued by the Spanish crown. That policy forbade shipping to or from the colonies except in Spanish hulls and also forbade sales to any nation but Spain. The monopoly insured extra dividends at home but was a constant irritant to the colonists, who needed more—and cheaper—manufactured goods in return for their exports of silver, hides, tobacco, sugar and spices than Spain was able, or willing, to supply. Moreover, the colonists wished to sell their goods at the highest possible price, not at that set by the home country's monopolists.

The second type of activity—freebooting—was the eminently practical process of letting the Spaniards find the booty and then taking it away from them. Freebooting was particularly attractive to younger sons of landed gentry who were prevented by the laws of primogeniture from inheriting property but who were not prevented from inheriting a taste for the world's goods. It was passably profitable for a number of years, but it took a resourceful freebooter named Giovanni da Verrazano, the discoverer of New York Harbor, to widen the eyes of the business community. Verrazano, a Florentine in the service of Francis I of France, saw his chance in 1523 and cut out from the Spanish fleet two of the ships carrying home part of the vast treasure the conquistador Hernán Cortés had seized from the coffers of Moctezuma, the Aztec ruler of Mexico. The loot was fabulous: gold, emeralds, pumas, cloaks and pearls; the weight of the pearls alone came to 680 pounds.

The freebooting business boomed almost immediately. In 1553, the French raiders, François ("Peg-Leg") le Clerq and Jacques de Sore, showed the way to such notorious Englishmen as John Hawkins and Francis Drake. De Sore, a belligerent Huguenot, went too far: when he captured Havana, he and his crew costumed themselves in priestly garb and capered around the cathedral, desecrating Catholic objects of worship. The Spanish did not forget. Ten years later when they captured the French colony in Florida, they killed the entire male population. This demanded further vengeance; in return Frenchmen later hanged the Spanish occupants of the same settlement.

THE freebooters succeeded at one time or another in capturing all the richest towns from Panama to San Juan in exploits that have made lip-smacking reading for adolescents of later years. The residents learned to retire to the hills when foreign sails bloomed on the horizon, taking as many of their valuables as they could carry. Then they would bargain for the ransom of their city and wait for yellow fever or dysentery to drive off the invaders.

The 16th Century ended with the three powers at a standoff in the Caribbean. England and France had taken nothing permanent, but their unchecked trading and raiding in the area did not help Spain's bargaining position when the series of 16th Century European wars came to

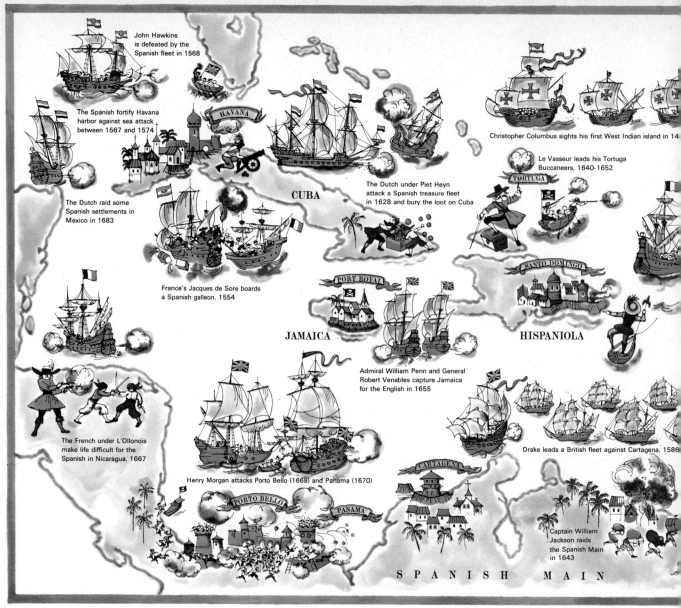

John Hawkins is defeated by the Spanish fleet in 1568

The Spanish fortify Havana harbor against sea attack between 1567 and 1574

The Dutch raid some Spanish settlements in Mexico in 1683

HAVANA

CUBA

Christopher Columbus sights his first West Indian island in 14

Le Vasseur leads his Tortuga Buccaneers, 1640-1652

TORTUGA

The Dutch under Piet Heyn attack a Spanish treasure fleet in 1628 and bury the loot on Cuba

France's Jacques de Sore boards a Spanish galleon, 1554

PORT ROYAL

SANTO DOMINGO

JAMAICA

HISPANIOLA

The French under L'Ollonois make life difficult for the Spanish in Nicaragua, 1667

Admiral William Penn and General Robert Venables capture Jamaica for the English in 1655

Henry Morgan attacks Porto Bello (1668) and Panama (1670)

Drake leads a British fleet against Cartagena, 1586

CARTAGENA

PORTO BELLO

PANAMA

Captain William Jackson raids the Spanish Main in 1643

S P A N I S H   M A I N

PLUNDERING PIRATES turned the Caribbean into a battle-ground during most of the 16th and 17th Centuries. Hawkins and Drake, later to be victors over the Spanish Armada, first gained the favor of their queen, Elizabeth I, by filling the royal coffers with gold extracted from Spain's ports and galleons. The infamous Morgan and the gentlemanly Penn continued to

a close. In the Treaty of London of 1604 and in the 1609 Truce of Antwerp, by which Spain recognized the independence of Holland, the British and Dutch won a historic concession: they agreed to respect—they said—the Spanish monopoly of trade in Spain's established colonies but in turn were to be allowed to trade in those parts of the world not effectively occupied by Spain.

It was the Dutch who dealt the decisive blow to Spain's commercial hegemony in the area. The Dutch depended more heavily than either the French or the British on foreign trade, and

when their Portuguese salt supply was cut off by Spain's annexation of that country, they turned to the New World. A shortage of salt may not seem important enough to warrant sending fleets on six-month voyages across the sea, but the basic Dutch cargoes, fish and meat, could be preserved—in those days before refrigeration—only with salt. Cross the sea they did, making as many as two sailings a week for years. Their new source of supply was a bleak salt flat near Cumaná, Venezuela. Naturally, shipowners did not dream of dispatching ships with empty hulls on the outward voyage, and

FREEBOOTING IN THE CARIBBEAN

"Peg-leg" le Clerq urges his men to attack Spanish Hispaniola in 1552

Spouting defiance, John Hawkins goes looking for Spaniards in 1567

Dashing Sir Walter Raleigh accepts a bit of tribute while raiding Trinidad in 1595

TRINIDAD

relieve Madrid of money and islands. And, like bees attracted to a golden honeypot, seafarers from France and Holland buzzed about, attacking the Spanish, the British and each other.

so they, too, joined in the smuggling trade.

The expansion of Dutch overseas commerce was helped by the establishment of a Dutch West India Company in 1621. The company was given the right to settle, build, administer and defend its properties and was granted a trade monopoly on the coasts of West Africa and the Americas. Soon the organized fleets of the company were making systematic attacks on Spanish shipping while engaging in a profitable three-cornered trade, bringing European manufactured goods to West Africa, slaves to the West Indies, and sugar, salt, hides and other products of the islands back to Europe.

The Dutch became colonizers only after being traders and were not as interested in establishing colonies in America as they were in looting the Spanish silver fleets and in the slave trade. Nevertheless, between 1630 and 1640 they added Aruba and Bonaire to Curaçao as part of their growing overseas empire, and they annexed the tiny northern islands of Saba, Sint Eustatius and Sint Maarten.

FROM the earliest days, there was a flow of disappointed settlers on their way home, and some of these—Englishmen driven off their tobacco plantations in South America by food shortages and by attacks by the Spanish and Portuguese—became, about 1625, the first settlers of the eastern Caribbean islands. They planted and harvested the exotic produce that grew so easily on the islands—dyewoods, cotton, spices and tobacco. The arrival of these goods on the European market caused such excitement that it became relatively easy to raise money for new colonizing expeditions.

By 1631, there were 4,000 rough and hard-fisted new Barbadians growing maize and tobacco, and the English, already established on St. Kitts, were moving into Antigua, Montserrat, Nevis and part of St. Croix. Most of the workers were indentured, i.e., under contract to work without pay for from three to seven years in return for ocean passage. At the end of the contract period, if they lived, the laborers in addition were to receive land of their own.

In many ways indenture was worse than slavery; a slaveowner expected to use his property for a lifetime while a contract holder had to get his return quickly and therefore was likely to work his laborers harder. But despite the appalling conditions, the indentured laborers continued to arrive; by 1640 the population of Barbados had jumped to 30,000, and St. Kitts and nearby Nevis held another 20,000.

When Oliver Cromwell assumed power in England in 1653, he decided to gain a West Indian empire for the English by driving papist Spain from the islands altogether. He ordered a fleet assembled under the command of Admiral William Penn (father of the founder of Pennsylvania) and an army organized under General Robert Venables. The expedition of 2,500 men landed at Barbados and made off with 4,000 "volunteers"—many of them indentured servants still under contract—and so much food that the island was all but ruined. Another 1,200 men were recruited from the smaller islands, and the whole mob, largely untrained, descended on Santo Domingo, capital of Hispaniola.

THE attack was a fiasco, and only flight back to the ships saved the invaders from a massacre by the Spanish cavalry. Penn and Venables decided in the freebooting tradition to attack Spanish-held Jamaica. This was successful, since Jamaica possessed no defenses to speak of. Cromwell thought it a poor substitute for Hispaniola, but he did not scorn it, and the island was never recaptured by the Spanish.

Paradoxically, there were periods of cooperation between Europeans in the Caribbean. For a time the French and the English amicably shared St. Kitts. The French were led by Pierre Belain d'Esnambuc, whose ship had foundered on the beach in 1625 after losing a battle with a Spanish galleon. The English were having trouble with the local Carib Indians and D'Esnambuc agreed to help. The two groups divided the island, the British in the middle, the French on the ends. When the French got their ship repaired, the produce they took to France was enough to inspire the formation the following year of a colonizing company called Compagnie de Saint-Christophe. It was not an immediate success. The Spaniards descended on St. Kitts in 1629 and blew up everything in sight. The colonists scattered, some of them to become the nuclei of colonies on other islands. Others returned and replanted their crops, and St. Kitts was soon flourishing again.

A few years later the French established colonies on the big, fertile islands of Martinique and Guadeloupe. Both islands changed hands between the French and the British six times, eventually winding up under French control. A new governor general, Phillippe de Lonvilliers de Poincy, built a stone-and-brick palace on St. Kitts and methodically annexed Saint Barthélemy, St. Croix and half of St. Martin. When the board of directors decided he was getting too self-important, they sent out a replacement, but the newcomer was driven away by gunfire. Various private owners to whom the company sold its rights subsequently operated the French islands until 1664, when the French West India Company was founded, with the French crown as its largest stockholder. The French West India Company took all the possessions for itself. Ten years later, Louis XIV abolished the company and took over the colonies. In 1713, France lost St. Kitts to England, but earlier, in 1665, the French West India Company had begun the systematic colonization of Saint-Domingue, the colonial name for Haiti, which was to become France's richest colony.

LARGE-SCALE settlement of Dominica, the rugged island between Martinique and Guadeloupe, and of St. Vincent, farther to the south, was delayed by the resistance of the warlike Carib inhabitants. In 1748, England and France agreed to neutralize the two islands and leave the Caribs in possession, but French settlers slowly gained a foothold on each—only to be dislodged by Britain a decade after the agreement. W. Adolphe Roberts, one of the most entertaining historians of the West Indies, notes that though the Caribs found the French the tenderest of all Christians they had eaten, the French bore them no ill will and in fact got along better with the Caribs than other Europeans did. There was, however, a bloody massacre of Caribs by the French on Grenada, which ended, according to legend, with the remaining Indians' suicide in a mass jump from a cliff now known as Carib's Leap.

Thus an uncertain proprietorship of most of the islands was established by the second half of the 17th Century. Meanwhile, with the olive-skinned peoples native to the region practically eliminated, the black-skinned ones imported from Africa were rapidly populating the islands.

Vigorous surf, flashing brilliant blue and white, rushes up an inlet near Luquillo, a beach resort on the coast of Puerto Rico.

Gemlike Islands Riding a Limpid Sapphire Sea

As with the mythological Pandora and her box, Columbus opened a world of greed and strife when he discovered the West Indies. Piracy, slavery, war and tyranny deeply scar the islands' history. But despite human evil, the islands themselves were always a demiparadise of golden beaches and abrupt green hills, washed by the unsoilable sea and smiled upon by the impartial sun. The centuries of suffering and anguish have not dimmed the area's natural glory.

CRYSTALLINE WATER reveals the swirling outlines of the coral reefs and sandbanks that lie between some of the tiny islands off the coast of Great Exuma Island in the Bahamas. The limestone and coral of these riverless specks of land yield little silt to cloud the water, and the brilliant colors made by sand and water extend over much of the 750-mile length of the

Bahamian archipelago. Coral reefs, which are formed by the accumulated skeletons of tiny marine creatures, are found everywhere in the Caribbean, and many beaches are made of the fine white sand produced by the erosion of the coral. The Bahamas extend north of the tropics, but they lie athwart the Gulf Stream and share the warm seas of the more southerly islands.

Two customers and a merchant preparing bananas for sale attend the quayside market which flourishes in Willemstad, Curaçao.

BUSY HARBOR STREET in Port-au-Prince, Haiti *(opposite)*, leads from a run-down hill district called Bel Air *(foreground)* to the waterfront with its crowded wharves and cargo boats.

GOSSAMER NETS hanging up to dry are strung between small fishing boats on the beach at Bellefontaine, Martinique. Fishing is an old industry in Martinique and employs some 2,000 men.

A weary ox hauls a cart of sugar cane to a processing mill in Trinidad as a car whizzes past. Sugar production is being modernized

on some islands, but laborious and primitive methods survive.

3

The Impact of Slavery

TWO opposite but equally dramatic developments are taking place in the Caribbean, both working toward the reduction or elimination of color divisions among the dark- and light-skinned peoples of the islands. One is occurring on the Spanish-settled islands of Cuba and Puerto Rico and in the Dominican Republic; there, color lines are vaguely drawn and the whites generally accept the lightest-skinned people of mixed parentage as social equals—and as marriage partners. Census reports state that the "white" population of these islands is growing, the Negro population shrinking.

On the islands settled by the British, Dutch and French, on the other hand, the proportion of Negroes and of "mulattoes"—descendants of slaves and Europeans—is approaching the 100 per cent mark. A significant number of these islanders of course have more than one European ancestor, and their complexions are light, but the remaining members of white society refuse to accept them as equals. The latter are finding, however, that their white skins are sometimes a handicap. It is not uncommon these days for them to remove themselves entirely from the islands, particularly from newly independent Trinidad and Jamaica, where government jobs are gradually being filled by the darker-skinned citizens.

IN part because of these developments, a distinctively new society is being born, one that is neither "European" nor "African," but West Indian. In order to understand the origins of this still-developing culture, it is necessary to look at the bitter intimacy in which the peoples of the Caribbean lived for 450 years and at the forces which brought them together. If any single factor predominated, it was the ruthless pursuit of profit through the cultivation of sugar cane in the 17th, 18th and 19th Centuries. Europeans had known—and treasured—the taste of sweetness long before there was enough for everybody. There was only an uncertain supply of fruit crystals, honey and the sticky brown product of Asiatic and Spanish cane sold as sweets and medicine for the very rich. There were no such things as sweet drinks or sweet candy for the general public. Although the Spaniards understood the value of the crop—they had established a mill in Hispaniola within 14 years of Columbus' landing—they concentrated on their mainland colonies and did not undertake large-scale planting in the islands until the 19th Century.

Sugar was therefore still in short supply in the mid-17th Century when the French and English colonists, who had been concentrating on tobacco planting, faced the fact that fine Virginia tobacco was driving their inferior island strain off the market. Looking around for a more profitable crop, they began to think seriously about sugar cane. Climate and soil conditions on their islands seemed favorable; a few early plantings in Barbados had grown well. On the other hand, the yield from the Barbados crop had been low—and the cost of installing a mill, which they referred to by the Spanish term *ingenio,* seemed prohibitive.

At this point Dutch merchants, always on the hunt for cargoes for their big ships, lent a hand. They had learned how to handle the crop in Brazil before they were driven out by the Spanish and Portuguese, and they now were able to show the British planters where mistakes were being made and how profitable it could be to correct them. The Dutch also offered credit on big crushing-rollers to be turned by wind, water or animal power; heavy copper vats for boiling and crystallizing; distilling equipment for turning molasses into rum; and hoops and staves to be made into great hogsheads for storing and shipping the dark, moist crystals. It remained only for the planters to turn their acreage to cane.

THE Dutch predictions of profit came bountifully true. As early as 1657, an observer concluded that yearly net profits on Barbados were running about $75 per acre. A plantation of 500 acres, a common size, could at that rate expect to turn about $37,500 profit per year in the money of the day. Thomas Modyford, later governor of Jamaica, started planting in Barbados with the avowed intention of returning to England with half a million dollars. He died in Jamaica before attaining that goal, but other planters achieved similar ambitions. Sugar became so ubiquitous that it was used as a medium of exchange between the Dutch traders and the planters. (It was valued at a penny a pound; the value of money in those days may be reckoned by comparing this with modern sugar prices in boom years, which have gone as high as 23 cents a pound.) A broad-brimmed hat could be bought for 120 pounds of sugar in 1651; a pound of brown thread for 40 pounds; men's shoes for 16 pounds; a yard of white Osnaburg linen, the basic material out of which slave clothing was made, for 6 pounds.

During the 17th Century, the story of the Caribbean was largely the story of the cultivation of sugar in the British and French colonies, and the story of sugar in those islands is the story of slavery, for the cane harvest required large numbers of strong men to wield the cutlasses or machetes and to haul the cut cane away. While the supply of European indentured labor was running out, apparently inexhaustible numbers of Negro slaves were available—the Portuguese had been purchasing them in West Africa for more than two centuries. If the English colonists felt any qualms about making use of the institution of slavery, they dispelled them by the simple expedient of deciding that Africans were a morally and biologically inferior species, and that they were in fact "slaves by nature."

It is impossible to say when the first Negro set foot in the New World; there may even have been one or two with Columbus' first expedition. At any rate it was not long afterward that the Spanish Crown granted a license to a Spanish nobleman to import slaves to the West Indies "provided the slaves be Christians." Enormous numbers of Africans eventually reached the New World — some estimates run as high as 20 million. Mortality was high and the birth rate far too low to maintain the slave population, but it was easy to get replacements, at first from the Portuguese traders and later from other entrepreneurs.

The first foreigner believed to have intruded on Portuguese slave territory in West Africa was the English adventurer John Hawkins, who in 1562 persuaded some London businessmen to back him, outfitted three vessels, sailed to the Guinea coast and, in the words of the 16th Century English geographer and historian Richard Hakluyt, "got into his possession, partly by the sword and partly by other means, to the number of 300 Negroes at the least."

TERMS FOR RACIAL MIXTURES

One result of the mingling of Negroes and Caucasians in the Caribbean was the creation of a new group of persons of mixed parentage. Technically the word "mulatto," which the islanders used to describe this group, means only a person with one Caucasian and one Negro parent, but it is still widely used to designate a person descended from any mixture of the two races, however many Negro or white ancestors he may have. Since many of the islands differentiate between Negroes, Caucasians and this third group, the term has been used where necessary in this volume. Other terms, no longer used, were invented to describe exact proportions: quadroon for the offspring of white and mulatto, octoroon for the offspring of white and quadroon, mustee for the offspring of white and octoroon, and mustefino for the offspring of white and mustee.

Hawkins' sales methods were equally effective. Sailing illegally into a Spanish Caribbean harbor with cargoes of slaves, he would make formal request for permission to trade, pleading that he had been blown off course and adding that he did not wish to resort to force. Local officials in the ports of Isabela, Puerto Plata and Monte Cristi, all on the north coast of Hispaniola, conspired with him to make their acceptance of his terms look like capitulation to a well-mounted British attack. In return for his three shiploads of slaves, Hawkins took home five shiploads of hides, ginger, gold, silver and pearls.

The method of supplying the traders with slaves, once the trade started in earnest, makes a sorry tale of greed and cruelty, involving African tribal kings and village chiefs as well as Europeans. It was established practice for tribesmen to enslave prisoners of war and to sell them. But after slave prices began to rise, wars degenerated into mere raids. When the temptations became great, the greediest local kings resorted to selling their own tribesmen. The unfortunate captives were marched to "factories" on the coast—grim stone forts that did double duty as slave prisons—to await eventual sale to traders and shipment overseas.

The transfer of slaves to traders sometimes took months. The prices asked by the trader on his diverse cargo of kettles, cloth, grain, guns, tallow and hides had to be set against the value of the slave, which was determined by such factors as size, sex, health and tribal origin. The haggling, therefore, was interminable. Iron bars worth 50 cents to $1.50 each were common trade items, according to the historian Hubert Herring. They became a kind of currency. At the beginning 10 bars would buy a prime slave, but later 80 or 100 bars were needed. The cost of feeding the cargo on the weeks-long "middle passage" (the second leg of the three-cornered trade) averaged $2.50 per slave in locally obtained cassava flour, yams, plantains, grain and fish. Losses from various frightful diseases and suffocation in the sweltering holds averaged about 5 per cent and reached 20 per cent on unlucky crossings. But once in the colonies, a healthy slave brought about $50 in the early days and as much as $500 in the 19th Century. At either time the percentage of profit was extraordinary.

Under good conditions, investment in a slave could repay the cost to the planter many times over. According to one 17th Century account, the work done by a slave paid his purchase price in a year and a half. The advantages were enormous. Upkeep was nominal, for on many plantations slaves were expected to cultivate their own kitchen gardens in their spare time—usually Saturday afternoons and Sundays—and to raise most of their own food (occasionally they were given a taste of imported salt fish or meat). Clothes were minimal. Slaves were required to build their own wattle-and-daub huts. Thus the planter's heaviest outlay was not for his labor but for his mill equipment which, with extended credit, he was able to amortize over the years. His land was his by grant, and sugar could grow in soil too exhausted for other crops.

ON the other hand, sugar could be a tricky business. Competition from a more productive island could drive prices down—many of the Caribbean military skirmishes were basically raids to destroy a competitor's mill, burn his fields or abduct his slaves. Other hazards included slave revolts, blights and hurricanes. Many planters were constantly in debt, living from one harvest to the next on expensive loans with the knowledge that crop failure could mean bankruptcy.

By the second half of the 17th Century, the slaves outnumbered their owners on most of the islands, and many of the males captured as adults had been warriors; here and there among them were former village chiefs. Mutinies, bloody uprisings and escapes occurred from the earliest days on Hispaniola. In Barbados the first rebellion took place in 1649. In Jamaica whole plantation households were slaughtered or poisoned and many runaways vanished into the hills. On Hispaniola the richest years were terminated by the slave revolution of 1791-1804 and the resulting extermination of the remaining whites, a revolt which brought the republic of Haiti into being. Everywhere existed a common form of protest—suicide—which was fostered by a slave legend that all deceased slaves would be reborn in Africa.

TO discourage rebellion, the colonists took every possible precaution. They stocked their plantations with slaves from different tribes to prevent easy communication between them and kept them uneducated and ignorant. On the British and Dutch islands the colonists forbade even religious instruction, denied the right of legal marriage and sold children separately from their mothers. Punishments were of the utmost savagery; a visitor to Jamaica in 1707 described the penalty for rebellion as nailing the offender to the ground with crooked sticks and then applying fire by degrees, starting with the feet and hands and gradually working up to the head, a procedure "whereby their pains are extravagant." For lesser crimes, the slaves were castrated or had half a hand or foot chopped off with an ax. For running away they were forced to wear heavy iron rings on their ankles, rings with pendent iron hooks around their necks, or spurs in their mouths. For "negligence" they were suspended by the hands and flogged until they were dripping with blood.

European investors were increasingly worried about the possibility of slave revolts. As early as 1685, France promulgated the famous Code Noire. It prescribed severe penalties for slave offenses but granted slaves a number of rights. They were entitled to trial, to minimum

SUGAR REFINING, as it was practiced in slave times and afterward, is shown in this 1855 engraving of a boiling room. The equipment consists primarily of a row of iron caldrons set into masonry. The juice pressed from the cane by the rollers (*background*) flows into the first caldron where it is boiled and then is passed to the next. By the time it has reached the last caldron it is sufficiently purified to crystallize.

quotas of food and to a degree of family security (children were not to be sold separately from their parents). The code also established punishments for the murder of slaves and for making sexual attacks upon them. Freed slaves were granted equal rights with persons born free. The Jamaican slave law granted similar rights, although not until a century later. It added that owners were required to care for old, disabled or sick slaves and to see that slaves were taught Christianity. Owners were to suffer the death penalty for murder of slaves and other penalties for lesser brutality. The law also forbade slaves to gather for dances or other nighttime meetings (explaining that intoxication was injurious to their health), to "pretend to supernatural power . . . to promote the causes of rebellion" or to strike any white person.

THE English and Dutch generally thought of slaves as more or less inanimate property without legal status. They made it extremely difficult for the slaves to become free, obtain education or have anything resembling family life; when emancipation came, the slaves were as unprepared for freedom as the colonial societies were to absorb them. The English and the Dutch had had virtually no experience with the institution of slavery before the exploitation of Africa; having enslaved the Negro, they illogically allowed the fact of his slavery to convince them of the Negro's inferiority.

Spanish colonists, on the other hand, tended to think of slaves as people who had suffered a misfortune, and slaves in the Spanish islands existed in a healthier psychological climate. The scholar Frank Tannenbaum in his persuasive book *Slave and Citizen* describes the status of the slaves in the Spanish colonies as legal rather than moral. Spanish slave law, which dated back to Roman times, permitted the slave a number of doors to freedom: among other things, he could buy it (even on the installment plan) or he could win it by saving his master's life. Moreover, once freed, a former slave was entitled to all the rights of a man born free. There was, as a result, from early times, a sizable population of truly free Negroes and *gente de color*, or "people of color," in the Spanish colonies. Thus the way was paved at the beginning for the subsequent relatively easy relations between races and colors. The treatment of slaves in the French colonies was somewhat better than in the Dutch and English colonies, but considerably less humane than in the Spanish.

The Africa from which the slaves were removed boasted a number of separate cultures that endowed their members with distinctive characteristics. Various colonists of the New World, when contemplating slave purchases, favored members of different tribes or nations according to characteristics which they ascribed to them, and their selection may to some extent have contributed to the various personalties of the separate islands. The Spanish preferred the strong Yorubas of western Nigeria. The English thought the clean-limbed, intelligent Ashanti and Fanti from the Gold Coast were best, although they also believed that these people were "more prompted to Revenge, and murder the Instruments of their Slavery." The French favored the Dahomeans (Whydahs) and partially peopled Saint-Domingue with them, along with the powerful Congolese and the Ibos, although the last were said to be suicide-prone. For house slaves, the French preferred the gentle Mandingoes. They employed a greater number of house slaves than colonists on other islands. A wealthy Saint-Domingue planter and his wife might have six personal slaves apiece and their children three. One great house of the 17th Century was served by 40 slaves. In the French and to some extent in the Spanish islands, favored slave girls became the confidantes of colonial women, who told them their intimate secrets and who listened in turn.

IT was the propinquity between owner and slave which brought the far-reaching changes to the islands that we have already noted. Miscegenation created a third group, that of the "mulatto," or colored people. These people were distinguished from the Negroes in the islands. Because the mulattoes were so often born free—or freed by the father's specific order—they gradually began to invade the white man's enclaves, sometimes obtaining education, property and even slaves of their own. The fact that they were barred in many areas from full participation in the white-dominated economy and society, however, contributed to social difficulties which have yet to be fully overcome in the islands.

In the British, French and Dutch areas these people of mixed parentage still occupy a carefully differentiated social position between the black and the white. In the Hispanic islands, there is less certainty about where to draw color lines, with the result that the barriers between white and nonwhite are more fluid, a point developed by the stimulating Dutch anthropologist Harry Hoetink in his study of race relations in the Caribbean islands, *The Double Image*.

Ways in which slaves and their descendants were affected by their associations with white Europeans are easily seen. The slave peoples learned foreign languages and in time developed out of them their own Creole languages. Eventually, they adapted Christian religious forms to their own African-born religions for day-to-day solace. They came to develop a fierce sense of personal independence, yet when they achieved political independence they adopted European forms of government as a matter of course.

THE Europeans, too, reacted to the propinquity. In the islands, European class notions were overlaid by a color-caste structure. People were separated into levels determined by the color of their skin: white, "colored" and dark. Within these were subdivisions and overlapping based on economic factors. The slaves were, as a matter of course, divided into two major groups: house servants and field-workers. The whites by social practice, and sometimes by legislative action, were divided into several groups: large and small landowners, who were also the voters and the legislators; propertyless urban business and professional people; merchants and laborers; and poor whites. This rigid stratification, although somewhat obscured today by the gradual reduction of color divisions, can still be seen in the West Indies.

Together, the islanders evolved a lilting style of speech; West Indian Spanish and French are often as picturesque to visiting Europeans as "calypso English" is to Americans. Europeans contributed their melodic style to the creation of a West Indian music also noted for its African rhythms. Today, out of the clash and cooperation of both groups, the islanders are reaching an understanding of their own identity as West Indians—an understanding which they must have before they can successfully mold their own destinies.

Sugar-field workers run toward sheds for protection as a squall heads down the slopes of Mount Misery on the island of St. Kitts.

Old Economies Existing Side by Side with New

Too many of the West Indian islands are still shackled by economies essentially unchanged since the days of slavery. Some of these islands are small and lack the resources necessary to do more than grow a few crops and raise livestock. On them backbreaking labor and small wages remain the rule. Other islands, however, where vigorous development programs have attracted new industries and new trade, provide models of what energy and investment can achieve.

SWEATING LABORERS attack a lush stand of sugar cane on St. Kitts, an island whose economy is almost completely dependent on its crops of sugar and cotton. The cutters must hack through the thick stalks near the ground, trim off the leaves and cut the cane into convenient lengths with heavy machetes. For this hard labor the cutters get $1.90 a ton. The other field

hands, who gather the cane and load it in carts, get less. Each acre of cane field on St. Kitts yields an average of more than 30 tons a year and some 15,000 acres are under cultivation, but 62 estates must share the $13.5 million this crop yields in exports. Thus little filters down to the field hands in wages. As a result, the average income on St. Kitts is only $190 a year.

BRIGHT PENNANTS bedeck a pontoon bridge in Willemstad, the capital of Curaçao, and give a festive air to the Dutch colonial buildings which face the Breedestraat, a busy shopping street. Willemstad and other communities across the bay share a fine harbor which handles great quantities of cargo. The area refines and transships large amounts of Venezuela's crude oil.

VAST REFINERY near Willemstad, owned by the Shell Oil combine, works into the night as a tanker loads *(above)*. Curaçao ships petroleum products to the U.S. and other countries.

COMFORTABLE CLUB, much patronized by Shell employees and their families, overlooks Piscadera Bay near Willemstad. Used as a resort hotel, the club has tennis courts and a pool.

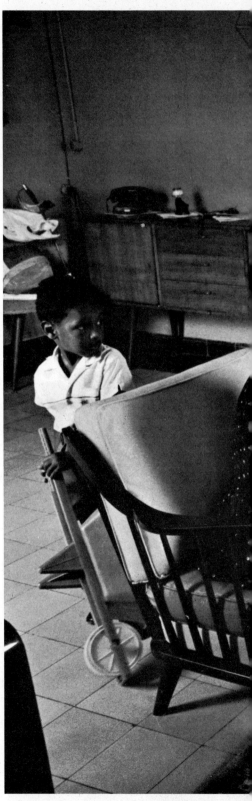

WELL-EQUIPPED KITCHEN with ample working space makes life easier for Mrs. Simon as she and her young niece, preparing dinner, talk with Mrs. Simon's two-year-old son, Ildefons.

RELAXED AFTERNOON in their comfortably furnished living-dining room (*right*) is enjoyed by the Simons (seated on the couch) and their neighbors, Mr. and Mrs. Aquiles Bronswinkel.

TELEVISION WATCHING quiets Ildefons and his older sister while Mr. Simon studies charts of the refinery where he is employed. The oil industry is generally stable and layoffs are few.

Edgard Simon reflects the high living standard made possible by Curaçao's industry

A "vodou" altar in Haiti, decorated with paintings, is littered with sacred objects, including a cross, bottles of the liquors favored by

"vodou" gods and an electric fan to cool the dancing worshipers.

4

Solace from an Unseen World

WHEN the first Spanish conquistadors waded ashore in the West Indies, they took possession in the name of God and the Crown. The Crown was King Ferdinand and Queen Isabella. Their God was the Judaeo-Christian God, whose earthly representative was the Pope and who demanded unwavering faith, but who promised in return life after death. Their world was set about with mystery and peril—they were completely ignorant of many of the main features of its geography—but it was also filled with gold and adventure, and in search of these the physical mysteries could be ignored. The Spanish adventurers lived dangerously, achieving miracles of endurance under conditions of unbelievable hardship, but they were sustained by their hopes of wealth and by the certainty that death was not final and that suffering on earth was but a prelude to happiness in the hereafter.

The postponement of many of its benefits did not make this faith any less satisfying to the white man. He had been raised to think in abstractions and metaphors, and he was able to take comfort in promises of a distant reward and to imagine a single deity, infinitely powerful but infinitely remote. To the African, on the other hand, the spirit world was nearby and was densely populated by deities who directly controlled various aspects of the physical world. His gods, like those of the ancient Greeks, resembled humans. They controlled such concrete matters as rain for crops, victory in battle or success in love. Like the Christian, the African approached the world of the spirit through men of specialized knowledge and experience, and he showed his piety by performing certain public duties and by obeying certain moral or ritual precepts. Also like the Christian, the African could, through study and sacrifice, himself become a priest. But here the resemblance between the anthropomorphic and pragmatic faiths of the Africans and the formal dogmas of Christianity came to an end.

THE Catholic Church was at the pinnacle of its glory and power during the early days of the Spanish Empire. The proud Spanish Crown deferred to it and helped it to grow as powerful in the New World as it was in the Old. The Inquisition itself crossed the Atlantic, and its tribunals in Peru and Mexico tried and often caused to be put to death such heretics as Portuguese Jews and Dutch and English Protestants. But out on the island barricade the Church was less secure. Distances were too great and the common people too scattered to permit efficient administration of the faith. The slaves on the Catholic islands were baptized, of course, for their salvation was a fundamental rationalization of the slave traders and owners, but their instruction in the faith was sketchy and was often resisted by the owners on the grounds that any kind of education could inspire rebellion. As the centuries passed and the West Indies sank into apathy, the Catholic influence became severely attenuated.

The decline of Catholic power has continued even in recent years. In Cuba, the Church's criticisms of the Castro regime were answered first by vituperation and then by the ejection of most foreign priests from the island. In the Dominican Republic, Catholic denunciations of the villainous Trujillo dictatorship brought no noticeable improvement in the regime's policies. In Puerto Rico, the Church was not sufficiently powerful to imperil the re-election of Governor Muñoz Marín, even with the threat of excommunication for any Catholic who voted for him—a threat that was never carried out.

EXISTING always alongside the white man's religion has been the African's belief in spirits—invisible powers who may be deities, souls of the dead, or the animate personalities of such inanimate objects as trees and stones. The extent and intensity with which this belief is accepted range from full-formed religions to a vague superstition not unlike that of the skeptical American who still declines to walk under ladders and builds his skyscrapers without 13th floors. A mild form of spirit worship is practiced, for example, by dwellers in rural areas when sickness strikes and the doctor is days away. Even people who consider themselves good Catholics then seek aid from the spirits. The popularity of such spirit worship is considerable. Even in Americanized San Juan, spirit mediums do a brisk business, and potions and charms are manufactured in modern factories. In all parts of the Caribbean area, there are people who would hesitate to launch an amatory adventure, take a step in business or allow their daughters to marry without calling in the local version of seer—variously called a lookman, teacher or sleeper, depending on how he contacts the spirits.

There are times, of course, when the seer will be unable to relieve sickness or misfortune, and more daring treatment is called for. In cases where the trouble may have been caused by black magic in the employ of an enemy, the only remedy is to summon what the Haitians call a *houngan* or *bocor* (witch), and English-speaking West Indians call an obeahman, whose magic is stronger than that of the enemy.

Because even the highly developed spirit religions have no organized dogma or theology, it is sometimes hard to distinguish them from this casual belief in spirits. But in the case of Haiti, there is no question: *vodou*, or voodoo, is a true folk religion. It offers its followers solace in the face of the hostility of nature and the inevitability of death, and it explains the mysterious orderliness of the universe. It provides the Haitian peasant, as it provided the slave, with a rich and vivid imaginative life that permits him to withstand the severe reality of his existence. On the cultural level it resembles other religions, being a repository for the transplanted Africans' creative instincts—for music, dancing, painting, carving.

DURING the early colonial period, the only feature of *vodou* to draw the attention of the French Catholic planters was the dancing. They thought it rather quaint and folkloric and surrounded by a few harmless superstitions, and they sometimes gathered of a Saturday night to watch the show. But the "superstitions" turned out to be far from harmless, for *vodou* helped make possible the successful Haitian slave rebellion of 1791. It is said that *vodou* drums telegraphed the call to battle from plantation to plantation, and it was from *vodou* that the slaves took inhuman courage, convinced that their guardian spirits made them invulnerable. Even so, *vodou* might not have become the religion of the entire population but for the fact that in 1805 General Jean-Jacques Dessalines, the ruler of Haiti, decreed separation of church and state and then expelled all but a handful of Catholic priests. By 1860, when a concordat was signed and a number of priests returned to Haiti, *vodou* had seized the imagination of the people.

In the easygoing way of a folk religion, *vodou* had long since adapted some of Catholicism's features to its own purposes. The cross represents the crossroads, a significant *vodou* symbol, and also the cardinal points of the compass. Certain prayers at the beginning of a *vodou* ceremony bear considerable resemblance to Catholic prayers. A number of Christian saints can be identified among the *vodou* spirits, which are called *loa*, and the Christian God Himself is accepted as a distant and powerful *vodou* god.

The Catholic missionaries' campaign to reconvert all of Haiti after 1860 was a nominal success. The Haitians saw nothing wrong in attending Mass after the *vodou* ceremonies were over, and the priests made themselves, for the moment, equally adaptable. James Leyburn, in his important book *The Haitian People*, suggested what a *vodou* credo would be like, if there were one: " . . . I believe in the efficacy of sacrifice; in the pleasures of living; in respect due to twins; in the careful cult of the dead, who may return to our abodes; in the spiritual causation of diseases and misfortune; in the dance through which we may be 'mounted' by our *loa;* in the possibility of interfering with the normal flow of events by means of magic; in the efficacy of charms and spells, and in the Holy Catholic Church."

THE aspect of *vodou* that is most difficult for outsiders to understand is the phenomenon of "possession," which enables Haitians to see and speak to the spirits who run the world. Possession has been observed, studied and written about by psychologists, sociologists, anthropologists and common travelers. William Seabrook was one of the first in the field with his superheated ("blood-maddened, sex-maddened, god-maddened") book, *The Magic Island.* The photographer and moviemaker Maya Deren claimed she actually experienced possession and described it in compelling detail in *Divine Horsemen.* The anthropologist Alfred Métraux (in *Voodoo*) and the sociologist Leyburn have studied it with scientific detachment.

All of these descriptions of possession have in common a strange matter-of-factness, as if the spirits, these elusive intangibles, were as observable as the dancers' movements. The subject enters a trancelike state (usually after undergoing convulsions), during which one of the *loa* enters his or her body and "rides" it. The human personality is displaced by the superhuman, the human features take on the characteristics of the spirit's (masculine or feminine, good or evil, old or young, crafty or honest), and the human throat utters the *loa's* words, some of them in wholly unintelligible "tongues." The possession may last minutes or hours or sometimes days, during which time the person invaded by the spirit is fed the spirit's favorite food and drink (often things quite impossible for unpossessed humans to consume) and offered his favorite diversions. Afterward, the human remembers nothing of his behavior as a god.

It should be noted here that the phenomenon of possession, while little understood, is or has been a part of Christianity as well as of many other religions throughout the ages. Various revivalist cults in the United States retain versions of it. Some of the earliest Christians held feasts during which worshipers underwent ecstatic religious experiences—experiences that were soon found to be incompatible with the smooth operation of organized theology.

The *vodou* ritual begins in a subdued fashion. It may include the lighting of candles and the sprinkling of water on the ground. Then, as the drums—which have summoned the people to the ceremony—pick up their beat and the dancing starts, a chicken, a goat or a bull may be sacrificed and the desired *loa* is beseeched to enter the human. Most of the ritual takes place in a "peristyle" with walls that reach two thirds of the way to the ceiling and a decorated central post down which the spirits enter. The ceremony is a tumultuous, earsplitting event. In addition to the two or three powerful drums, there is a chorus whose strident

falsetto chanting sounds like chaotic improvisation, but which is actually a disciplined performance. Above everything rise the commanding voices of the *houngan* (priest) or *mambo* (priestess) and the *houngenicon* (leader of the choir).

The invocation of each spirit is accompanied by its own prescribed rituals: the drawing on the floor of his *vèvè*, an intricate design that helps bring the spirit down to earth; the blessing and dedication of sacrificial animals and offerings of food; and finally the ritual drumming and the uninhibited dancing that culminate in the arrival of one of the spirits.

Vodou possession has been compared to the psychological state of hysteria. Some particularly susceptible believers may be seized unexpectedly anywhere, but it ordinarily takes the combined stimuli of occult practices, ritual sacrifice and the physical-psychological impact of the drums to bring it on. Physically, the drums create air waves which buffet the bodies of all who are near. Psychologically, they hypnotize by repetitions and variations of complex patterns of sound and rhythm. First the drums and voices create one set of vibrant patterns. Then suddenly there comes an intrusive shift which upsets the stable dimension of the rhythm and drives the dancers into such confusion that some of them stop for a moment and mark time, men turning to statues, women flapping their white skirts. After that, the rhythmical shifts arrive more and more frequently and even the moments of relative stability are shattered by brutal hammer blows on the biggest drum. This relentless attack eventually becomes focused on one or more dancers, staggering them again and again, each blow

---

SOME POPULAR "VODOU" GODS

ERZULIE is the eternal female, combining muse and mistress. She is always pictured as fabulously wealthy, with gorgeous jewels and robes.

BARON SAMEDI is associated with death, but he is also both comic and arrogant, affecting horn-rimmed spectacles, top hat, frock coat and cane. He also loves ribald songs, obscene jokes and erotic dancing.

LEGBA, a spirit who guards gateways and crossroads, is always invoked in *vodou* ceremonies because without his permission the other gods could not enter the temple.

DAMBALLA is a spirit whose symbol is the serpent. He is sometimes compared to St. Patrick, who is also associated with snakes.

---

further loosening their grip on reality until finally their own consciousness is pushed aside and the *loas* take over.

Strangely enough the drummers, who are so intimately involved in the *vodou* ceremony, are not priests but simply believers who are professional musicians. The drums themselves, however, are sacred objects, blessed when they are made, propitiated during the ceremony (the dancers kiss the ground and pour libations of rum before them) and hung up carefully in the temple after it.

ALL Haitian ceremonial drums have a family resemblance, being segments of tree trunks hollowed out by chisels or fire and with one end covered by a hide stretched to the desired tension by a system of pegs and cords. They are played by the fingers and palms, and some are swatted with pistol-shotlike results by thin sticks or hammers. The basic drum orchestra has three: the big *maman*, which speaks with a mellow and rather mournful baritone; the *segond*, smaller and higher-pitched; and the still smaller *boula*. The two smaller drums between them keep up a rippling, muttering conversation in strict but extremely complicated rhythms. There are subtle differences between the many drums used for different types of dances, but one is unique—the *assòtò*, which stands so high that the dancers must leap into the air to beat its head with sticks.

Some *vodou* dances are devoted to a family of gods from Africa called *Rada;* others summon the *Pétro loas*, some of whom are spirits added in the New World. Still other types include the *Congo* spirits who are summoned by a rhythm that has become the basis of a popular West Indian dance.

The hierarchy of spirits is literally endless, as new *loas* are constantly being added and the attributes of the older ones change slightly from time to time and place to place, exhibiting qualities as various as the nature of human beings. Any of the spirits may enter a body at any time, but several are very popular and are frequent visitors.

Some of the *vodou* religion's outstanding characteristics—such as possession, ritual dancing and animal sacrifice—are also features of cults in other islands: the *Shango* of Trinidad, named after the Yoruban thunder god; the Cuban *santería* and the Jamaican *pocomania*.

Occupying an area somewhere between developed religion and the black magic of obeah, the ancient African beliefs and practices relating to death survive undiminished. Because of the relative nearness of the spirit world, where departed souls join the *loa*, there is always the possibility that the spirit of a dead man may return to cause trouble. Even worse, a man thought to be dead may have his soul captured by an evil *bocor* (witch). He then becomes what Haitians call a zombie and the British West Indians call a *jumbie*. The danger of this is that the undead creature is quite helpless against the *bocor* and may be put to cruel labor or to evil pursuits. Zombies are recognized by their dazed expressions and their servility.

TO ensure against such dire possibilities, the first step is to be certain that the deceased is really dead; in some areas the bereaved will shoot the corpse in the head or poison it. If the dead person has ever been possessed by a *loa*, the bond must be broken and the deity freed. To accomplish this the priest ducks under the sheet that covers the corpse, shaking his rattle in its ear, muttering charms and invoking the *loa*. Suddenly he calls the deceased loudly by name, whereupon the corpse slowly raises its head or shakes its shoulders as if trying to sit up—some say it is all done by the priest— and then slumps back forever. A more elaborate procedure is advisable on the death of anybody who has been gifted in the arts or professions. Because these talents are considered precious and useful, a ritual is performed which, it is believed, transfers the deceased person's spirit to a living man.

Further steps are required to protect the living from the dead and to give the freed soul of the deceased its chance to become itself a deity. These include a proper funeral, for a spirit that is not correctly mourned may remain in the vicinity and take to evil. The neighbors respond enthusiastically to the first wails of the bereaved, for the key to a good funeral is a good wake. While the next of kin keen loudly and occasional laments are raised by friends, the others eat and drink, tell stories, sing songs and play games to help the dead body's spirit enjoy its last hours on earth.

The burial takes place before dawn after the body has been taken to the cemetery speedily and by a devious route to confuse the spirit about the way back to its house. Subsequent rites during the following months and even years vary from island to island. They often include a ninth-night ceremony and sometimes a 40th night, both of which combine elements of Christian and African beliefs.

THE gap between basically African ceremonies such as ritual dancing and basically Christian ones such as hymn singing is bridged by Trinidad's Baptist Shouters cult, which still functions despite a history of official disapproval. The anthropologists Melville and Frances Herskovits spiritedly describe Shouter services in *Trinidad Village*. The ceremony takes place in a shelter that resembles a *vodou* temple, but the music is the rawboned Sankey and Moody hymns sung at American revival meetings. The first verses are sung tentatively and without variation. Then the tempo picks up, the offbeats are emphasized by handclaps, and the melody slurs away from the rigid old tune as some of the singers try their own variations while others start vocal imitations of drumming ("ram a-ba-ram"). Excitement rises until some members of the congregation become possessed and dancing and shaking are general. The spirit of the Shouters is eloquently expressed by a Shouter who spoke to the Herskovitses: "When the body is fill with joy, it move, it shake. If I got up one mornin' an' didn't feel like shoutin', then I know the Lord is not with me. I would know something was wrong."

It is characteristic of the colored peoples throughout the West Indies that they accept with equanimity the presence of strange or alien cults—the Hinduism and Mohammedanism of the East Indians, the Buddhism and Confucianism of those Chinese not converted to Catholicism, the Greek Orthodoxy of the Syrians. Nevertheless, there has been a certain amount of religious intolerance and persecution on the islands, usually the result of either the personal policies of colonial administrators and dictators or Catholic pressure on the lawmakers. In 1917 the British rulers of Trinidad decreed that nobody could play drums between the hours of 10 p.m. and 6 a.m. without a license from the police. Naturally this law discouraged a whole family of celebrations from *bongo* dance to *bélé*. In Haiti, the Church set about stamping out *vodou* with an antisuperstition oath, *la renonce:* " . . . with hand on the gospels I swear never to give a food-offering of whatever kind, never to attend a [*vodou*] ceremony of whatever kind, never to take part in a service to a [*loa*] in any way whatsoever. . . ." In 1940 the Church launched a more intensive campaign to destroy drums and such other *vodou* objects as talismans and sacred trees. This was most successful in the rural areas. Everywhere it resulted in reconversions to Catholicism and, sometimes with even more enthusiasm, to Protestantism. (Shakers and Pentecostalists both undergo a religious trance that the Haitians found comfortably familiar, while the more staid Protestant faiths, which were increasing in number, were rumored to give better protection than Catholicism against the reprisals of vengeful *loas*.)

IT was to be expected that the increase in prosperity and literacy throughout the area—with many of the schools run by various churches—would make the descendants of African slaves more susceptible to the writings and teachings of Christianity. Missionaries of all cults are everywhere, and they seem to be getting results. It remains to be seen, however, whether in time of need the religiously modernized West Indian will resist the temptation to consult a seer.

Jamaican women take part in an obeah, or black magic, ceremony. Belief in witchcraft and black magic is common in the islands.

An Amazing Variety of Sects, Faiths and Cults

Religious groups of every sort flourish in the West Indies. Most of the islands are predominantly Christian, but the Christians are divided into dozens of sects ranging from such formal bodies as the Roman Catholic and Episcopal Churches to gospel singing revivalist groups like the Shouters of Trinidad. On some islands, where part of the population has roots in the Orient, there are significant numbers of Buddhists, Moslems and Hindus. Haunting all the islands is a lingering belief in spirits and magic that the slaves brought with them from Africa generations ago. Most exotic of all West Indian faiths is the transplanted African religion called *vodou*, or voodoo, which, with its violent, hypnotic rituals, has captured the imagination of virtually all the people of Haiti and has offshoots on some of the other islands.

BEGINNING A CEREMONY, *vodou* worshipers pray before a complex and handsome *vèvè*—a symbolic drawing—of a bull. As the ceremony progresses, the worshipers will begin to dance to drum music, and later a bull will be sacrificed. During the dancing, some of the participants may enter a trance in which they are "ridden" by a god who was summoned to appear.

OCCULT RITUALS that lead to "possession" are at the center of Haiti's "vodou" religion

ENTERING A TRANCE, a girl writhes as she becomes possessed by a *vodou* god. While in this state, which may last many hours, she will assume all the characteristics of the deity.

SLEEPING BY AN ALTAR, *vodou* worshipers lie in their temple in obedience to a commanding spirit. Paintings of sacred animals and trees cover the walls of some *vodou* temples.

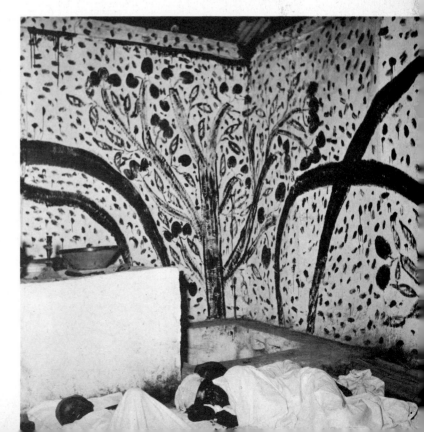

JEWISH SYNAGOGUE of the Mikveh Israel congregation, built in 1732 in Willemstad, Curaçao, boasts a dignified and rich interior. Reputedly the oldest synagogue still in use in the Western Hemisphere, it has a floor covered with sand to symbolize the Jews' 40 years in the desert. The congregation was founded in 1656 by Sephardic Jews expelled from Brazil.

CATHOLIC PROCESSION led by four women carrying a large icon of the Virgin Mary files down a side aisle of the Cathedral of Our Lady of Guadalupe in Ponce, Puerto Rico. Although there is religious freedom in Puerto Rico, and Protestant missionaries are both numerous and busy, the Roman Catholic Church predominates with some 85 per cent of the population.

5

A Dormant Heritage Awakened

THE story of artistic creation in the West Indies is the story of the reawakening of the ancient African heritage after four centuries of hibernation in a strange land. But this artistic impulse reawakened in forms quite different from those it had taken in Africa. When the slaves were taken to the New World, they were separated from their native ways of life and had no choice but to emulate what they could observe of the white colonists' cultural pattern. This led many of them into a tragic acceptance of the Europeans' conviction that Africans were inferior and immoral and their customs degrading. The growing number of people of mixed parentage, who renounced the African element of their background in their struggle to be accepted by whites, reinforced the black man's sense of inferiority and of lost identity.

It is not surprising under these circumstances that dark-skinned West Indians felt little esthetic urge. When their descendants did start to create, in the modern awakening in the Caribbean, they had no choice but to use European languages and European artistic forms—the novel, the poem, oil painting and strophic songs. In matters of style and content, however, their originality frequently overpowered these European influences. Their most successful creations are neither African nor European but distinctly West Indian.

The West Indians' talent for design revived earliest in Haiti, where slavery and colonialism were first eliminated. On the brown earth of the temples, the *vodou* priests drew with astonishing skill and imagination the symbolic *vèvè* —designs which are the earthly representations of the *vodou* gods—and then, without regret, danced them into dust. Complex designs in color twined about the central column of the temples and enriched the barrels of the sacred drums, while on the streets festival celebrations brought forth bright banners and imaginative costumes. These creations were merely decorative, but they served to preserve instincts for design and color that were to emerge later.

IN other areas, however, the creativeness of the West Indian peoples had remained very much alive. Their first important aural creations were two languages of their own, French Creole and the Papiamento of the lower Dutch islands. The art of telling folk tales also blossomed as soon as these languages evolved. In the early days the tales, like the singing of familiar songs, brought the comfort of remembered things to people in distress. The Africans brought the Anansi stories with them on the slave ships—tales still told with relish. Anansi is a spider whose origin is buried in prehistory; in Gold Coast mythology, he appeared as creator of the world and stealer of the sun, but by the time he reached the West Indies he was a trickster who generally managed to triumph even though he tangled with such powerful foes as tigers. The same basic character is recognizable as Brer Nancy in Jamaica, Ti Malice in Haiti, B'Rabby in the Bahamas and in the southern U.S. as Br'er Rabbit, whose adventures were recorded in the Uncle Remus stories by Joel Chandler Harris. Whatever his guise, he was the underdog struggling against superior forces, a hero with whom slaves could identify.

Other characters, all fearsome, populate West Indian folklore: Papa Bois, master of the forest and enemy of the hunter; Maman de l'Eau, a relatively benign snakelike spirit of streams; La Diablesse, a frightful crone who puts on magical beauty and uses other lures not usually described in fairy tales to entice would-be Don Juans into predicaments both embarrassing and horrid. Still worse is the Soucouyant, or vampire, who sheds her skin and flies through the night to suck the blood of innocents. Potential victims may destroy her by finding her skin and sprinkling it with salt and pepper so that it will be too itchy for her to wear. (One variant of this imaginative tale is the basis for a ballet created in San Juan by a former pupil of the choreographer George Balanchine.)

Other West Indian stories have been built around real events in the lives of the people. A local news item may be expanded and interpreted until it embodies a moral or satirical point. Satire and stinging wit are twin talents of the experienced West Indian storyteller and he wields them mercilessly. The most highly prized tales, which provide amusement at the expense of someone else, often become the basis for songs. In places where one of these satirical songs is well known, the tune alone, whistled or hummed, is enough to inform bystanders that the tale applies to somebody who is passing by. This kind of raillery is close to the modern phenomenon of calypso singing, but before discussing calypso it is necessary to look at a development that shaped the musical personality of the entire West Indies: Afro-American drumming.

THE knowledge of how to make and play drums was fundamental to the Africans' spirit-worshiping religions. The drum rhythms of the *vodou* ceremony, like the drawings of the *vèvè*, were created to prepare the dancers for the arrival of the creatures of the spirit world and, on occasion, for the amusement of the visiting deities. Some of them evolved into the rhythms of the Latin American dances so popular today. The originals varied from what Alfred Métraux calls the "marvelously indecent" *banda* to the relatively polite shuffling derived from the white man's minuets and polkas.

West Indian dancing increasingly became a social activity and less strictly an adjunct of religion after the slaves were emancipated. The transformation parallels that of the U.S. Negroes' work songs and spirituals into jazz, although with important stylistic differences. On the mainland, the overwhelming influence of English-derived songs, marches and hymns stamped jazz with parade-ground meter and rigid melodic phrasing—handicaps that stimulated jazzmen to prodigies of invention. In the islands, on the other hand, the plurality of Negroes and the scarcity of European musical models permitted the "Afro" element to dominate. The strongest European influence, in fact, was a restrictive one: the fascinating—and, from the primitive point of view, obscene—practice of holding a partner of the opposite sex in close embrace, which effectively tamed the wildest liberties of the dancers. The musicians had to modify their approach; they were no longer drumming to inspire people to dance, but simply to accompany dancing. Melodically, the rhythm of the French and Spanish languages caused a sweetening and softening of musical shapes, most obviously by causing unaccented or "feminine" endings.

UNLIKE social dance music on the U.S. mainland, however, which until lately was limited to two rather formal rhythms (the "fox trot" with its walking four-four beat and the waltz with its three-four), the West Indian islands have a dozen rhythms and characteristic steps to match. The basic pulse may still be four beats to the measure, but the musicians subdue and overlay it with a wide variety of syncopations and manipulations of rhythm which specifically inspire movements of hips, shoulders and arms as well as feet.

Every major island has its own dances, which it claims jealously and proudly. Cuba, the biggest, produced the widest variety and gave the name "Afro-Cuban" to the genre. The Cuban dances range from the ancient and jungly *son* (rhymes with stone) and *guaracha*, in which even the fundamental downbeat is slightly displaced, to the more modern *rumba*, *mambo* and the humorous *cha-cha-cha*. (Modern subspecies such as the *pachanga* are bewilderingly numerous and are more likely to get themselves born in the Spanish-speaking parts of New York City than in Cuba.)

TO set up the welter of rhythm required by these dances, drums are basic. Among the most familiar West Indian drums are the tall *conga* and the paired, lap-held *bongos* played by the bare hands. Other rhythm instruments include the serrated gourd called the *güiro*, which is scratched by a wire brush to sound like a fast steam locomotive, and the seed-filled gourds called *maracas* that rattle when shaken. Unoccupied members of the orchestras' wind sections may thicken the clatter by tapping odd objects. When a band is in the steamy deeps of a *guaracha*, it is not uncommon for all the musicians to stop blowing and start knocking while dancers advance and retreat, hips and legs fluid, arms bent and swinging prize-fighter fashion, shoulders and heads steady.

Puerto Rico has, besides the Cuban dances, its own ebullient *plena*, a simple folk rhythm punctuated frequently by random explosions on the drums. The *plena* usually has lyrics which, like the Trinidadian calypso, deal with actual events and personalities. Both Haiti and the Dominican Republic claim to have fathered the sinuous, graceful dance called the *meringue* in French and *merengue* in Spanish, in which each new downbeat, following a playful and propulsive preparation on the drums, is left unexpectedly empty. In Martinique and Guadeloupe, where the Parisian influence is strong, the dance is the *biguine*, which bounces along on a current of tumbling but quaintly civilized drumming as if the missionaries had put a Mother Hubbard on the rhythm.

All these variants are lively and often have lyrics made up of alimentary or baldly sexual jokes. Sentiment is reserved for the *bolero*, the Latin American ballad form in slow fox-trotlike tempo. Some *bolero* melodies are sophisticated, but most of their lyrics are as tortured as the lovers' protests that they purport to be.

The most widely admired of all the music to come out of the West Indies is the Trinidadian calypso, a body of amusing and often insolent songs sung by the men who made them up. The singer-composers often give themselves grand, high-sounding names like Lord Protector, Mighty Sparrow or Small Island Pride. Their lyrics are a waterfall of polysyllables and incredible rhymes and deal with real people or events in Trinidad—often in scurrilous terms. True calypsos were usually sung in a dialect so obscure that no outsider could hope to understand them, but when the commercial value of calypso became apparent, the most astute calypsonians began to compose cleaned-up lyrics and to sing in more intelligible English. These calypsos sound rather like misaccented and earthy patter songs by Gilbert and Sullivan.

The roots of calypso are both sacred and secular. The earliest singers, called chantwells, were court jesters to the lawless colonial barons and also acquired heroic, semilegendary status among their fellow Negroes. By 1880 the influence of their songs had become so great that the words were sometimes believed to have supernatural power. Occasionally the leading chantwells and their followers engaged in fierce battles with the stick-wielding votaries of rival singers. Later the chantwells restricted themselves to all-night verbal "wars," the victors being the quickest-witted singers who could taunt and insult each other for hours without pausing or missing a note.

MEANWHILE, in a separate movement, the Carnival of Trinidad was developing. Originally it had been the Catholics' "farewell to the flesh," a period of license celebrated on the Monday and Tuesday before the beginning of Lent in many parts of the Christian world. In Trinidad's colonial days, when society was dominated by French émigrés, Carnival was decorous enough, if surviving accounts are to be believed. Carnival then included masked dancing, music in the streets and certain unspecified but undoubtedly rude "pranks." Of special interest, in the light of later developments, was the torchlight procession in blackface called *canboulay* (from *cannes brulées*, or "burned cane"), patterned after the processions of slaves on their way to fight fires in the cane fields. Freedmen were permitted to wear masks in the streets, but slaves were not.

EMANCIPATION marked the transformation of Carnival into a "lower-class" event, in which mobs of dark-skinned people in masks and costumes made the streets dangerous. "Bands" in uniform costume were organized, each one devoted to the depiction of a historical scene or to farcical pantomime of living personages. Masked harlequins and blue devils prowled the streets, which reverberated with raucous and earsplitting music. Observers reported being shocked by the "hellish scenes," the near-nudity, the uproarious noise and the emphasis on obscenity.

Disorders increased with every Carnival, and the government finally forbade demonstrations before Sunday midnight, the beginning of Lundi Gras. Even this did not restore order, for on the stroke of 12, large *canboulay* bands, their members armed with 6-foot sticks, emerged from the slums. They were led by brazen-voiced chantwells who bellowed musical challenges at each other. This led to numerous and bloody pitched battles. In the *canboulay* riots of 1881, 38 policemen were injured in fights with the bands. After that, the bands were forbidden to carry sticks, and the harlequins were tamed somewhat by regulations against scenes of obscenity and transvestism. Another new law forbade parading before 6 a.m. on Carnival Monday, a moment still known as *jouvé* (possibly derived from *jour ouvert*—i.e., daybreak). Besides, the streets were being paved, thus covering the stones that had too frequently been used as missiles. The upper classes began to feel free to join the fun once more.

Today, Carnival grips all Trinidad in an annual shudder of ecstasy. Islanders who might find themselves elsewhere at Christmas would not dream of missing *jouvé*. The Monday and

Tuesday before Lent are not legal holidays, but business grinds to a standstill. Streets tremble under bands of several hundred marchers, all in colorful costume. Dancing and marching continue for 42 hours, driven by the thumping, humming and syncopated clangor of giant steel bands. Deaths from Carnival are rare today, but contusions are common, and girls join the march at their own risk. Almost equally ecstatic carnival celebrations occur on several West Indian islands, but Trinidad's remains the most colorful.

Calypso is the musical core of Carnival in Trinidad. During the weeks preceding the event, calypsonians test and polish their latest compositions before crowds that circulate the town judging the singers and the new songs. Early Tuesday morning, the tune judged by common consent to be the best is suddenly heard everywhere, played by dozens of marching steel bands, and its composer is acclaimed Calypso King for the year.

The musical impulse of the West Indians cannot be stifled by adversity or even repression. Trinidadians invented steel bands, for example, to take the place of banned African drums. A steel band is composed of different-sized "pans" made from the ends of 42-gallon oil drums. The barrel is cut short or left almost full length, depending on whether the instrument is to be treble or bass. Individual notes are produced by striking various segments of the head which have been "tuned" by careful hammering. A band of a dozen or more players sounds like a cross between a Mexican marimba and a giant mandolin.

IN Jamaica, where the bumptious calypso beat has been softened to a languorous "mento" rhythm, and in the Hispanic islands, percussive bass notes are often supplied by the *marimbola*, a resonant box on which the player sits while twanging the tips of flat metal springs mounted against the box's sides.

The lack of interest in classical or concert music in the West Indies can be attributed in part to history. At the time the Caribbean culture was settling into fixed patterns, the only concert music being performed in public in Europe was primitive opera and, in churches, organ and choral music. The Stradivari craftsmen were still perfecting their violins, and most wind instruments could produce only a few notes and those unreliably. Furthermore, few European artists bothered to visit the islands until the late 19th Century. In short, the West Indies for centuries had little contact with the mainstream of Western music. Of native musicians, the U.S. public will probably recognize the names of Puerto Rico's pianist Jesús María Sanromá and her Metropolitan Opera basso, Ernesto Diaz, and Cuba's composer Ernesto Lecuona (best known for "Siboney," "Malagueña" and "Andalucía"). In the less refined world of musical entertainment, dancer Geoffrey Holder and pianist Hazel Scott, both Trinidadians, are familiar to American audiences, along with a cluster of band leaders of Cuban and Puerto Rican antecedents specializing in West Indian and South American rhythms.

IN the present cultural and political awakening, concert music is being studied, written and performed. Puerto Rico's Casals Festival, begun in 1956, has given rise to an active conservatory of music in San Juan. But listening to music for reflective pleasure requires a different type of leisure than is available to the mass of West Indians. Classical ballet is studied, but a truer expression of West Indian culture is derived from the vocabulary of native dance. Groups in British, French and Hispanic centers are exploring African and West Indian sources in a search for a language of movement closer to West Indian realities. Newly established television stations in the larger islands are stimulating activity in all the temporal arts.

In the field of literature, Haiti was again the leader. Soon after the declaration of independence in 1804, the intelligentsia began to turn out prose, poetry and scholarly works; during the next 150 years, no fewer than 5,000 volumes were published (many of them printed in France), giving Haiti the highest per capita publication rate outside the U.S. in the New World. The critic Edmund Wilson does not give this early output a high rating for originality or style, but notes that it went through most of the same stages as French writing during the same period. It was not until the late 1920s, with the publication of *Ainsi Parla l'Oncle*, anthropological essays by Jean Price-Mars, and the founding of *La Revue Indigène*, that Haitians turned to their own Negro folklore and the mysteries of *vodou* for inspiration.

One ripening factor, ironically, was resentment against the presence of U.S. Marines, who "pacified" the country from 1915 to 1934. Haitian feelings of protest were sublimated into wide-ranging literary efforts—novels, poetry, drama, essays, literary articles and folklore studies. The writers were young men of the educated class who, in the heat of discovering their Negro heritage, left home to live in the slums, studied *vodou* and sought to draw creative power from the very fact of being Negroes. The fierce pride that grew out of their discovery has spread among intellectuals throughout the West Indies and has been given a name—*négritude*—by the Martiniquan poet and statesman Aimé Césaire.

IN this burst of creativity came three novels of Negro peasant life by the brothers Pierre Marcelin and Philippe Thoby-Marcelin: *The Pencil of God, Canapé-Vert* and *Beast of the Haitian Hills*. All three were translated into English. No others have caused as much excitement, but at least until the mid-1960s writers continued to produce in Haiti, even though the demand for one of their books may have amounted to only a few hundred copies.

Césaire and V. S. Naipaul, a Trinidadian of Hindustani origin, are the most renowned West Indian writers, but others are challenging them. English-speaking intellectuals who consciously search for release from their "cultural slavery" have produced several notable authors. From Trinidad and British Guiana have come Samuel Selvon, the late Edgar Mittelholzer, Ernest A. Carr and Errol Hill. From Jamaica comes the novelist John Hearne, and from St. Lucia the poet Derek A. Walcott. The Barbadian George Lamming—who moved to London—speaks with marvelous success in the primitive man's voice. His *In the Castle of My Skin* and *The Emigrants* were both published in the U.S.

Volumes of distinction are also appearing in the fields of history and the social sciences, stimulated by increasing interest in local culture and by the encouragement of scholarship given by the University of the West Indies. The late W. Adolphe Roberts of Jamaica wrote several detailed books on Caribbean history in a pleasant tone of detached partisanship, while P. M. Sherlock of Jamaica and J. H. Parry cover similar ground with accuracy and authority. Trinidad's Premier Eric Williams is also a historian of attainments. His works include *The Negro in the Caribbean* and *Capitalism and Slavery*.

Much of the literature of the Hispanic islands has taken the forms of polemical writing and poetry. The best-loved political heroes were also poets and journalists, notably Cuba's José Martí, who died for his cause in the Spanish-American War, and Puerto Rico's libertarian father and son, Luis Muñoz Rivera and Luis Muñoz Marín. Negro themes, throbbing with the accents of African drumming, were distinctively rendered in verse by Cuba's Nicolás Guillén and Puerto Rico's Luis Palés Mátos. Read aloud, this quatrain from Palés' "Danza Negra" sounds like a syncopated drum solo.

> *Calabó y bambú*
> *Bambú y calabó.*
> *El Gran Cocoroco dice: tu-cu-tú.*
> *La Gran Cocoroca dice: to-co-tó.*

Haiti's literary renaissance had been going on for 15 years before anything comparable took place in the field of painting. Evidence of the hidden Haitian genius was discovered by an American artist, DeWitt Peters, who happened to spot some decorative painting on the door of a rural refreshment stand, between a Pepsi-Cola sign and a Coca-Cola sign, and recognized it as art—spontaneous, able and the product of nothing more nor less than someone's inner urge to paint and draw. The painter was Hector Hyppolite, a *vodou* priest by profession, who was to become the most famous of the many Haitian "primitives." In 1944, Peters established a combination gallery and art school in Port-au-Prince called the Centre d'Art, which soon became the artistic home of the "primitive" school. The primitive quality of these paintings lies in a naive and detailed approach to the subject—*vodou*, magic, folklore or village scenes—and in an innocence of such techniques as perspective and a love of unmixed colors. Tourists from cruise ships were dazzled by the blazing colors and charmed by the style, and bought what they saw. By 1950 the popular art movement in Haiti had grown enough to have developed rival groups of painters, and today it is showing signs of outgrowing primitivism altogether. Meanwhile the excitement it has generated has stimulated painting on the other islands.

PUERTO RICO'S art movement burst forth after World War II. In this case the stimulus was the new Institute of Puerto Rican Culture, a government agency set up to serve as a general protector of the arts. The institute sees to it that all construction, or reconstruction, in the historic zone of Old San Juan is in keeping with the area's antique architecture; publishes volumes of poetry and prose; stages drama and dance performances; holds an annual competition for the finest handmade guitars and mandolinlike *cuatros* (buying the winning instruments to lend to deserving performers); sends local musicians on concert tours of the island; and puts on shows of painting, sculpture and handicrafts. Through its efforts, artists have been sent to study abroad and a whole generation of painters has grown up, led by the abstractionist Julio Rosado del Valle and the more representational Lorenzo Homar and Rafael Tufiño. Posters of striking originality and prize-winning motion pictures have been produced by another Puerto Rican government agency, the Division of Community Education.

By contrast with these vigorous young movements, Cuba's is old and distinctly cosmopolitan. It has its fusty academy (San Alejandro) and its National Museum in Havana. Some of the revolutionary painters of the 1930s, such as Amelia Pelaez and Cundo Bermudez, are already considered distinguished elders. Fidelio Ponce and Carlos Enriquez are dead. The new generation is led by Mario Carreño and Wifredo Lam. Lam, a Cuban of African and Chinese ancestry, is not only today's artistic hero but a leading propagandist for Castro. He paints huge, frightening canvases evoking, in the words of Aimé Césaire, "the jungle, the swamp, the monster, the night."

WEST INDIAN architecture is faced with a series of special conditions, such as the prevalence of hurricanes, earthquakes and termites, the scarcity of local wood, and the climatic qualities of hot sun, dampness and, in many areas, brisk trade winds. Recent design is often adventurous but rarely distinguished and sometimes ugly; even the finest examples tend to be more interesting externally than internally. At the two extremes are the graceless concrete boxes characteristic of housing developments and the spacious, elegant proportions of an occasional luxury hotel.

Although it is possible to find old houses of charm and personality buried in city slums or behind a crumbling plantation wall, there is little architecture of historical interest on many of the islands aside from the astonishing fortresses and some of the masonry town houses of the Spanish colonial period. Notable exceptions are the wooden houses that were built in urban Haiti about 1900. These structures have tall, deliberately narrow proportions with fanciful grillwork decorating their gloomy verandas and pointed steeples that give them the air of bewitched cathedrals. Their perilous proportions leave the impression that, if only in one unassimilated area of creativity, the West Indian population has managed forcibly to express one of its fundamental attitudes—a desire to live dangerously.

ELDERLY SCULPTOR, Zoila Cajigas holds up two of his small, brightly colored religious carvings. Cajigas was Puerto Rico's leading *santero*—literally, saint maker—until his death, aged 110, in 1962.

BRIGHT FRESCO looms over the choir in the Episcopal Cathedral in Port-au-Prince. Executed in 1951 by a Haitian painter, Wilson Bigaud, it shows the wedding at Cana in a setting of Haitian village life.

New Confidence and Mastery in the Visual Arts

For centuries native art in the West Indies was almost entirely ceremonial. Decorated drums were used in religious rituals and gaudy masks and costumes enlivened the various carnivals— as they still do. But in recent decades, there has been a powerful awakening in the fine arts of painting and sculpture. Haiti especially has produced a group of "primitive" artists who have a surpassing sense of color and design. Encouraged by several Americans, notably artist De-Witt Peters, such painters as Hector Hippolyte, Rigaud Benoit and Castera Bazile have flooded canvases with stark and sensual forms. Inspired by the Haitians, the artists of other islands have gained new confidence to swell the flow of powerful, gay and peculiarly West Indian art.

The Right Reverend Alfred Voegeli stands in a room containing part of his fine collection. The works on his right include a metal sculpture

perceived the power of the island's artists

COMIC CANVAS by Alix Roy shows a miterlike crown perched incongruously on the head of a potbellied infant who holds a sign proclaiming him king of a carnival band from Bel Air.

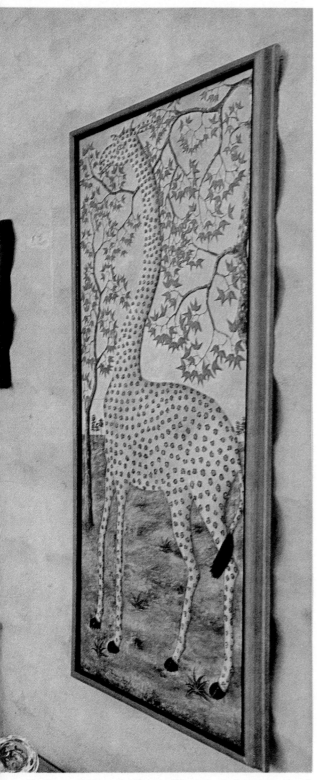

by Georges Liautaud. The giraffe painting is by Jasmin Joseph.

NAIVE FLOWER PAINTING on a table in the bishop's house is by Peterson Laurent, who was a blacksmith in a railroad yard until his recent death. His work is valued for its subtle colors.

BRILLIANT STILL LIFE dominated by a red snapper *(below)* shows the sophisticated brushwork of Enguerrand Gourgue, who though not a primitive nevertheless uses bright, flat colors.

*CARNIVAL brings out a
native genius for dance and mimicry
and a wild enthusiasm for
fantastic costumes and masks*

MASKED MARCHERS, billing themselves as *La Famille Co-chon,* or "The Pig Family," participate in one of the many parades that take place in Haiti on the days preceding Lent.

JOYOUS CROWD in Fort-de-France, Martinique, swarms about an absurd float *(opposite)* portraying an addled monarch in a giant shoe. Some 30,000 people fill the city at carnival time.

GROTESQUE HEADS of papier-mâché *(right)* are always a feature of carnival in Port-au-Prince, Haiti. The sign on the giant's hat reads *Le Cocus Imaginaire,* or "Imaginary Cuckold."

Their teacher playing policeman, a line of bag-toting school children files across an intersection in Fort-de-France, Martinique. Governed

by France, Martinique has 244 good public elementary schools.

6

The French Imprint

EVERY morning a plane from an island airline hops down the eastern Caribbean crescent. After a taste of American efficiency in St. Croix, Dutch practicality in Sint Maarten and British modernity in Antigua, the flight touches down at Guadeloupe, an island which seems to cling to an Old World past.

Not far from the airstrip is a swamp-locked port, smudged here and there from the days of coal steamers, and sheltering, among a flotilla of French merchantmen, a work vessel whose nightmarish superstructure of gears and conduits serves the purpose of dredging fill to make new land for housing. Pointe-à-Pitre, Guadeloupe's major port, demonstrates its participation in the 20th Century by a scattering of gleaming, geometric concrete structures, and out on the small island just offshore lies a pair of daringly designed tourist hotels. The airport runway is two miles long, to accommodate the daily intercontinental jets, but parked near the terminal are only the venerable, propeller-

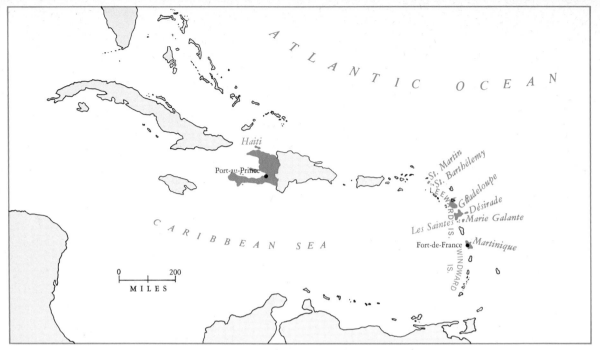

THE FRENCH WEST INDIES include French-speaking Haiti, although it gained independence in 1804. The islands still under French rule are concentrated in the Leeward Islands, where the largest is Guadeloupe. The other large island is Martinique, in the Windwards. Both Martinique and Guadeloupe are French *départements* and send representatives to the French legislature.

driven transports of Air France's local operation and the streamlined shapes of French-built light planes. Flight announcements for airline passengers are given in the seductive accents of metropolitan France. As the plane taxis out for take-off, the ominous slopes of Guadeloupe's volcano may be seen under the clouds that obscure the cone.

One hundred and twenty miles to the south, the first vista of Martinique from the air is of another volcano, Montagne Pelée. The setting sun illumines the deep gullies sliced into Pelée's flanks by rushing rivers of lava. The biggest trail of petrified lava points to the ruins of St.-Pierre, once the West Indies' brightest capital, where in 1902 a blast of fire crisped some 30,000 people in less than a minute and ignited vessels anchored in the roadstead. As the DC-6 slips down into Martinique's gathering darkness, the airport runway lights flicker into action; the island has a power shortage, and the markers are turned on only when needed.

Despite the distance between them—15 minutes by Boeing 727, a day or two by antique sailing vessel—Martinique is as French as Guadeloupe. The headlights of cars are amber-colored and their horns beep shrilly, like those of the mother country. Indeed, France's imprint is noticeable almost everywhere that the French touched in the West Indies. French Creole is the major language in St. Lucia and Dominica, which have been British for more than 150 years; French names and customs are common in Trinidad, which was a haven for French émigrés after the French Revolution of 1789; little St. Barts (Saint-Barthélemy), which was technically Swedish for the century preceding 1877, is as French as Martinique; pockets of Frenchmen retain their own language and customs on the U.S. island of St. Thomas, to which many French Protestants fled in the 17th Century. The French tone persists even in Haiti, which declared its independence from France more than a century and a half ago.

THE nature of the Frenchness is elusive. The outsider notices an indefinable sophistication; an easy approach to social relationships; an air of reasonableness that is nevertheless ready to explode into unreasonable passion, probably over that most unreasonable preoccupation, politics; a worldliness expressed in conversations in sidewalk cafés. The French quality nevertheless sometimes seems slightly spurious. Over the society of the French West Indies lies a faint smog of uncertainty—about personal security and about relationships with France and the world.

FOR a brief time in history, it appeared that France would impress its stamp on the entire Caribbean area. In 1782, France had taken all the British Caribbees except St. Lucia, Jamaica, Barbados and Antigua. That same year the French Admiral François Joseph Paul, Comte de Grasse, set out with a fleet of 35 fighting ships, 150 freighters and transports, and 6,000 troops to complete the conquest. But the redoubtable English Admiral George B. Rodney had arrived on the scene and, after a four-day pursuit, caught De Grasse off Les Saintes and smashed the French fleet. In the peace treaty, Britain got back all its islands except Tobago.

Within a few years fighting broke out again. This time, the British even managed to occupy Martinique and Guadeloupe. While they held the islands, Victor Hugues, an agent of the French Revolutionary government, managed a landing on Guadeloupe with a detachment of troops and set about liberating the slaves, employing them to help drive the British from the island and to massacre the royalist white colonists. But when Napoleon's General Antoine Richepanse arrived in 1802 to restore slavery in Guadeloupe, the Negroes were already back at forced labor, for they had been driven into the fields to keep the island's economy functioning. In the seesaw Caribbean fighting both Guadeloupe and Martinique changed hands more than once, but at the end of the Napoleonic Wars they were permanently assigned to France. Both soon returned to normal, which meant the somnolent, drifting normality of societies too shortsighted to see that the sugar bonanza had come to an end.

Plagued by labor shortages after the abolition of slavery in 1848, the many small plantations that failed were bought up and incorporated into the few giants that survived the ensuing years. Then in 1902, the cream of Martiniquan white society, which owned the great plantations, was snuffed out in the eruption of Montagne Pelée. Valuable plantations were buried in the almost simultaneous eruption of Guadeloupe's Soufrière. But the colored majority has never been able to overcome the political power of the remaining wealthy whites on either island—and that fact remains the key to an understanding of the social and economic problems which plague the islands to this day.

By the time of World War II, Martinique and Guadeloupe had become potentially explosive areas. When France fell, their joint administrator, Admiral Georges Robert, followed Vichy France. Britain and the United States were alarmed at the possibility that Germany might occupy the French West Indies, and suspected that German submarines were sheltering at Fort-de-France. They were also concerned about $2.5 million in gold which had been smuggled out of France in 1940 and deposited in Martinique. When diplomatic pressures failed to win Robert's cooperation, the Allies set up a blockade which caused severe hardship in the islands. Admiral Robert was threatened with military action by the U.S. and with rebellion by the populace, which was sympathetic to the Free French. The admiral resigned his command in 1943, allowing Martinique and Guadeloupe to join the Free French; food was landed by the Allies just in time to prevent starvation. But local problems remained acute, for there was no way to export sugar during the wartime shipping shortage.

IN 1946, Martinique and Guadeloupe (with its dependencies of Marie-Galante, Désirade, Les Saintes, St. Barts and the French part of St. Martin) achieved the status they had always wanted: they became *départements* (roughly equivalent to provinces) of France, politically equal—in theory at least—to the 90 existing *départements* of metropolitan France. Each of the *départements* is represented by three popularly elected deputies and two senators. They create an extremely small bloc in the French

Parliament. Actual power in the two islands lies in the hands of a Paris-appointed prefect who is "advised" by a locally elected council; the only locally elected officials with real political importance are the town mayors.

The system is similar to that under which metropolitan France itself is governed, but it is not popular in the islands. The small farmers and landless citizens who make up the bulk of the population are not, they feel, obtaining legislation which meets their needs. Prices, boosted by France's insistence on a trade monopoly, are high. Until recently exports—almost nothing but sugar, rum, bananas and pineapples—could be shipped only on French ships at premium charges. To import a non-French article is difficult and expensive (the tariff often exceeds 50 per cent). Duties are imposed even on some articles made in France, thus functioning as taxes on the consumer.

French West Indians in general agree that the great estates must be reduced in size to provide farms for more people. Land reform, they believe, might also encourage industrialization, if special benefits were offered to investors. Both land reform and industry have been promised repeatedly, but little land has changed hands and the growth of industry has been painfully slow. In Martinique, the big plantations are still owned by 15 or 20 white Creole families; Guadeloupe is more evenly divided among its citizens. Martinique's concentration of wealth also means concentration of political power, and the mass of Martiniquans is convinced that the *béké*, or landowners, are using their influence to resist the march of progress.

THE islands' economies do receive a boost from payments made under France's broad welfare programs, which constitute a considerable part of governmental income. Schooling is free until the student is 16, and the quality of teaching is high; the literacy rate is about 95 per cent. Medical care is also good, and practically free. Cases too complicated for local facilities are unhesitatingly sent to France. Best of all, as a citizen of France, each islander receives a monthly "living allowance," the amount depending upon such factors as wages and number of children. Such payments help the islands' 30,000 sugar workers through the idle months between harvests.

Inevitably, the islands' difficulties have bred political extremism and unrest. Many of the most respected politicians have been elected to mayoralties on the Communist ticket. Deputy Aimé Césaire, Martinique's most prominent citizen, deserted the party only after the brutal suppression by Soviet troops of the Hungarian uprising in 1956. Of the three major labor unions on Martinique and Guadeloupe, one is Communist, one is Roman Catholic and the third is moderately leftist. The three united in a strike for higher wages before the sugar harvest in 1963. Their goal was $3.80 a day; they attained about $2.20 (and later reached about $2.60).

MARTINIQUE'S man in the street believes that some important change will have to take place within the next few years. The change will, he thinks, be sudden, but not necessarily violent, and will probably result in increased autonomy for the islands. The Communists, among them in 1966 the mayor of Pointe-à-Pitre, call for independence.

In the meantime, the social patterns in the islands remain rigid. Although white and dark people mix with every sign of amity in business and society, no man identified as "colored," no matter how light his skin or how distinguished his position, ever enters a *béké* home.

Sociologists say that as the white Europeans leave West Indian society, their place in the top stratum will be taken by the lightest-colored group. This has already happened in Haiti, where the French landowners were destroyed along with their plantations in the bloodbaths of 1791-1806. The educated people of light complexion created a tightly limited society of some 200 families who called themselves the "elite." This class ruled the Haitian society and economy. Its members rejected all matters Negro, as if by ignoring their own heritage they could erase it. Peasant life, *vodou* and all kinds of manual labor were beneath contempt. Marriage was an almost exclusively elite custom—one Haitian definition of a member of the elite is a person who can claim five generations of married forebears. The society of the elite was marked by gracious formality and the tasteful display of classical French education. It was graced by some of the world's loveliest women. Secure in their class feeling, the elite lived austerely in their big, rather unkempt houses. Some of them never ventured out and received only members of their own ramified families.

IN recent years the elite have suffered a decline in prestige, but Haiti is still clearly divided between an educated urban group, most of its members descendants of slaves and Europeans, and the peasants, who are mostly Negroes. Like their counterparts in Martinique and Guadeloupe, the upper-class Haitians think of themselves as French, use the French language and behave with the casual sophistication of French people. The Haitian peasants are, on the other hand, a group apart. The grinding poverty that has faced them for four centuries has molded their composite personality.

Haitians are among the most gentle and optimistic of West Indians. When a peasant is asked about his health, he answers with wry honesty, "No worse, thanks." When his little garden yields more than enough to eat, he sends the surplus to market on his woman's head and with the profit buys such goods as hinges for his front door or fabric for clothes. Everything else, from mats to saddles, he fashions from grasses. He is fairly faithful to his common-law wife or wives (he may take another if he becomes relatively prosperous), and he is considered to be a good family man. But the Haitian is a mystery who continues to intrigue observers. One outsider has said: "I've lived among these people for almost twenty years and all I know about them is that I'll never really know them."

Haiti's social groups were already in conflict at the time of the slave revolt in 1791. Forming themselves into guerrilla bands, the slaves swept through the countryside, indiscriminately massacring both whites and *affranchis*—the freed descendants of slaves and Europeans, many of whom had acquired slaves and property of their own. The first and perhaps greatest of the slave leaders was Pierre-Dominique Toussaint (who became known as Toussaint L'Ouverture for reasons lost in the byways of folklore). A man of tremendous magnetism, imagination and military skill, he managed to rid the colony of every Frenchman with a claim to authority and declared himself governor.

Toussaint L'Ouverture restored order, halted the massacre of the *affranchis*, forced the freed slaves to farm the land and even induced a few white planters to return as administrators.

But the murder, torture and destruction were not yet over. Napoleon was ready to launch an American empire and felt compelled to begin by destroying the "gilded Africans" in Saint-Domingue. The French landed in 1802. Toussaint was plagued by treachery; after a three-month campaign the ex-slaves were routed, and he himself was shipped off to die in a French dungeon. The revolution was saved, however; yellow fever, an old enemy of invaders in the Caribbean, struck down the French army and its general. By then, the campaign had cost the lives of 50,000 Frenchmen and nothing had been accomplished; Napoleon quietly abandoned his plans for an American empire.

ON January 1, 1804, one of Toussaint's generals, Jean-Jacques Dessalines, assumed power, renamed the country Haiti (an Indian word for "mountainous") and declared it independent. Then he proclaimed himself emperor. He was a capable leader but proud and uncouth, and his two years of power were marked by cruelty and violence. He expropriated the old plantations, massacred the returned whites and decreed that all Haitian men would thenceforth be soldiers or fieldworkers bound to the land.

The imposing Henry Christophe, Dessalines' second in command, would simply have taken over the throne after Dessalines' assassination in 1806 if the *affranchis* in parliament had not rushed through a new constitution restricting the powers of the head of state. Christophe refused to accept the new order of things, but the *affranchi* forces compelled him to retire to the north. There, Christophe and his followers formed their own nation, while the *affranchi* leader, Alexandre Pétion, retained control in the south. Christophe proclaimed himself King Henry I, ennobled his lieutenants, established a pomp-and-circumstance court in a fairy-tale palace and built, on a mountain peak in the wilderness, a grim fortress, La Citadelle. Like his predecessors, he forced his subjects to work the land, and achieved such prosperity that when he died in 1820 (by his own silver bullet, so the story goes), his treasury contained more than six million dollars.

Pétion was by comparison colorless and ineffectual, but he is deeply revered for his democratic intentions. As a constitutional president, he initiated the land reform which is one of the roots of Haiti's economic problem today, doling out small parcels (down to 15 acres) to pay off his army. Freeholders refused to leave their own land to work on the remaining plantations, and squatters eventually took them over. Coffee replaced sugar as the dominant crop, for it could be made to turn a profit with less effort.

The next president, Jean-Pierre Boyer, reunited Haiti and then invaded the Dominican portion of the island, unifying Hispaniola for the last time; in 1844, the Dominicans revolted and re-established their independence. Boyer also obtained France's formal recognition of Haiti's independence and got the mother country to renounce all its claims against the young nation —in return for a promise that Haiti pay France a large indemnity.

SINCE then, most of the Haitian presidents have taken office by revolution, by coup d'état, by proclamation, or even—though rarely —by popular vote, and have subsequently left it abruptly for foreign sanctuary or oblivion.

By the beginning of World War I, Haiti was close to chaos and deeply in debt. France and Germany were threatening to collect their loans by force. There were three revolutions during 1914 alone. In July 1915, President Guillaume Sam slaughtered a jailful of political opponents and in return was torn to pieces by a mob. To prevent European intervention, the U.S. sent a force of Marines to occupy the country. They stayed for 19 years.

THE occupation was distasteful to everyone concerned, although, like some benevolent dictatorships, it did restore order. Public health services were established, and public works were built. But the Marines ran the country with such single-mindedness that a new rebellion broke out. From 1918 to 1922 the Marines waged a full-scale war against hill bandits called Cacos; some 6,000 Haitians were killed during the outbreak. The departure of the Americans in 1934 was one of the happiest days in Haitian history, although their leaving did not bring happiness to Haiti. Various attempts to unite the city workers, the peasants, the army and the elite failed with monotonous regularity in the ensuing years.

To most observers, Haiti's problems seem too enormous for solution. Financially in ruins from the almost continuous diversion of public funds, unable to educate or even to feed its bursting population of almost four million, the country is gripped by politicians whose hands are clenched as if in the spasm of electrical shock. In Port-au-Prince the lights go out every night for extended periods and the telephones are hopeless. In 1961, President François ("Papa Doc") Duvalier had his name placed at the head of all ballots in an election for the legislature, then after the balloting blandly announced that he had been unanimously elected to a second term. Later he declared himself perpetual president and continued a deadly police state regime in which few citizens dared speak their minds. Given the country's turbulent past and grinding poverty, Duvalier would probably not be the last affliction to be endured by the long-suffering citizens of Haiti.

Haitian farm folk pass a graveyard in Pétionville, a well-to-do suburb of Port-au-Prince, where a tomb bears a fresh, bright mural.

A Transplanted Gallic Charm and Instability

The former and current French possessions in the West Indies have, in varying degrees, two qualities long associated with France itself: civilized charm and troublesome instability. By far the most troubled is Haiti, which threw off French rule as long ago as 1804. A densely populated nation, Haiti is the poorest in the Caribbean area, and it has been plundered and terrorized by a string of tyrants. But in Haiti, as in the other French islands, people retain a soft-spoken courtesy that places them among the most sophisticated of all the West Indians.

HAITIAN LIFE, despite apparently hopeless economic stagnation and illiteracy, retains a pungent, exciting savor

FILIGREED PORCHES cover the façade of a tall, narrow frame house *(right)* in Port-au-Prince. This fanciful style of architecture flourished in Haiti about 1900.

TUMBLE-DOWN SHACK in the Bel Air section of Port-au-Prince *(opposite)*, still occupied despite its perilous tilt, is only too characteristic of the Haitian slums.

KALEIDOSCOPIC BAZAAR in Port-au-Prince *(below)* has booths selling fabrics and pans, clothes and carpets and, notably, chandeliers made of condensed-milk cans.

TYRANTS have long held sway in Haiti, preserving their power with costly forts and military force

MASSIVE CITADEL built in 1817 by the self-proclaimed king Henry Christophe crowns a mountain in northern Haiti *(opposite)*. Erected at the reputed cost of 20,000 lives, the fortress was intended to withstand a threatened French invasion. The French never came, but King Henry's subjects revolted and he committed suicide.

TENACIOUS DICTATOR, François Duvalier places his hat over his heart as the national anthem is played during military ceremonies in 1958. Duvalier has been kept in power since 1957 by a private force of armed thugs while his aides reportedly extort money from the people and Duvalier allegedly banks huge sums abroad.

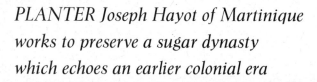
PLANTER *Joseph Hayot of Martinique*
works to preserve a sugar dynasty
which echoes an earlier colonial era

Hayot shares a continental breakfast with one of his

Working at his cluttered desk in the factory office,

FAMILY VISIT takes Hayot to call on his sister
(left), who lives in the house where Hayot was
born. The walls and floors are plain, but the house,
like many colonial structures, is large and airy.

two sons, Bertrand, who helps oversee the plantation.

Hayot reads mail as a native worker stands nearby.

FACTORY INSPECTION finds Hayot gazing at some troublesome pipes while his white-clad sons confer with a worker. Martinique's economy depends largely on sugar and its by-product, rum.

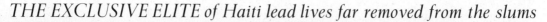

CHIC YOUNG WOMAN in a beehive hairdo watches a fashion show at the elegant El Rancho Hotel near Port-au-Prince. Light-skinned Haitians, descendants of the children of early French settlers and slaves, have long formed the nation's aristocracy.

SOCIALITE MODEL walks smartly across the El Rancho Hotel's poolside promenade in a fashionable Paris suit and hat. Many of these privileged Haitians are sent to France for their schooling and have impeccable Parisian accents and manners.

7

The
Disparate
British Islands

THERE is in the southeastern Caribbean
area a delightful culinary artifact called a
pepper pot. It was developed in the days before
refrigeration to preserve meat and poultry more
easily than could be done by smoking or salt-
ing; it survives its obsolescence because it tastes
so good. The food is put into a big kettle with
hot peppers and the juice of cassava root and
set on the back of the stove to simmer. New
ingredients are added as they come to hand
and the contents are eaten in small quantities,
so that the pot never becomes empty. The sim-
mering of years adds to the richness and savor.
A good pepper pot is so highly valued that it

may be willed from generation to generation.

The variety of elements present in the islands
once called the British West Indies would easily
qualify them as a Caribbean pepper pot, but
they have not yet blended to the point of pal-
atability. Proof of this was demonstrated in
1962 when the two big islands of Trinidad and
Jamaica and the eight smaller units of Barbados
and the Windward and Leeward Islands dis-
solved the Federation of the West Indies, the
incipient nation which was to have secured its
independence from Britain that same year.

There were many reasons for the federation's
dissolution. Despite their shared heritage, the

THE BRITISH ISLANDS form the most numerous group in the West Indies, but they are mostly small and make up only about one seventh of the total land area. Except for Jamaica and the Caymans, they form a 1,000-mile curving archipelago stretching from the Bahamas in the north to Trinidad in the south. Most of the islands have been British since the 17th Century.

British islands form neither a political nor an economic unit. Even geographically they are disparate, partly because of such natural reasons as variations in rainfall, and partly because of man's own meddling with nature. There is, for example, a basic difference between the flat, coral-built shapes of Barbados or Anguilla and the craggy, unkempt profiles and occasional black-sand beaches of most of the others, like St. Lucia and Dominica.

THE Caribbean islands frequently stir surprise and wonder in the traveler and sometimes a twinge of fear at the first realization that something solid exists in that liquid world. The feeling strikes voyagers when they realize that a blue cloud they have been watching on the horizon is really a blue mountain; it strikes people flying at jet altitudes when they find that a shadow on the sea is solid land. In both cases the voyagers are switched into a new frame of reference, as if a picture had suddenly jumped into focus.

Once ashore, the suspicion that there are other islands to be found—and that they will probably be sharply different from each other —tends to make people restless. So the early settlers of these islands, the pre-Columbian Arawak and Carib Indians, apparently felt as they pushed northward from South America to Trinidad and the islands which came to be called the Windwards. It was a long haul by dugout from Trinidad to Grenada, southernmost of the Windwards, but past that island the voyages were relatively short.

Today, of course, the journeys take less time. Once the rock north of Grenada known as Kick'em Jenny is rounded, the first of the Grenadines, a chain of 100-odd islets and reefs, swings into view. The 6,400 residents of the biggest, Carriacou, have divided most of the land and grow cotton and groundnuts on their small holdings. Carriacou, however, is not rich, and the young men sail away to find work or live on boats that keep them away from home for months. Crime is rare; a magistrate sails in four times a year from Grenada, holds court from 9 to 12 o'clock and leaves. Liquor is cheap, as it is in most of the southern West Indies, because the hundreds of coves and inlets are too good not to be used for smuggling, which is not considered much of a crime.

Almost everyone who has sailed through the Grenadines has thought of making one of them —perhaps Prune Island or one of the Tobago Cays—his own, perhaps to establish a guesthouse for which he would charge exorbitant rents, perhaps to build an airstrip for light planes or a marina for yachts; the schemes are endless. The islands north of Carriacou—the larger ones being Union, Mayreau, Canouan and Mustique—are dependencies of mountainous St. Vincent. The northernmost Grenadine, Bequia (pronounced Beck-wee), with Admiralty Bay providing deep-water shelter, is a boatbuilding and repair center where almost any day may be seen a 70-footer hove over on her side, careened in the age-old way to have her bottom repaired.

Over the horizon to the east of St. Vincent lies flat Barbados, once the lucrative pride of the Caribbean and one of the few West Indian islands to be occupied continuously by the British. It is still devoted almost exclusively to the growing of sugar. There is, as the travel books point out, some resemblance between the neat little lanes of Bridgetown and the rambling plantation houses of the country and the byways and manors of England. Outwardly the island's history has a smooth continuity, but inwardly Barbados has been restless; its people, polite to the point of subservience, have a bitter readiness to rise up and riot.

ST. LUCIA is the most picturesque of all the Caribbean islands. Its beauty reveals itself in the precipitous slopes of proliferating hillsides, the gardens that civilize some of them, the ever-shifting perfumes of the breeze that cools the capital of Castries, the long-limbed grace of the island's people. Yet the over-all effect remains ineffable, like the balance of a comfortable room or the face of a lovely woman. Dominica is less developed than St. Lucia, partly because it is more mountainous. In the right light, layer upon hallucinating layer of mountain profiles are silhouetted against each other, their outlines sometimes appearing to converge, as if the artist had become confused.

The British islands in the Leeward group north of Dominica are less dramatic. With its extensive flatlands, Antigua has become an important British airline base and U.S. missile-tracking station. Another asset, its profusion of inlets and sheltered coves, made it a headquarters of the British navy in the 18th Century, at the time young Horatio Nelson, on West Indies station, was learning the art of commanding a ship of the line. Little St. Kitts devotes most of its arable acreage to sugar, while Nevis, just three miles away, is its breadbasket. The Leeward chain tapers off to the northward, where Barbuda, Anguilla and some even smaller islands—all desperately poor—intermingle with Dutch and French possessions.

FARTHEST north in this chain lie the British Virgin Islands, a cluster of some 40 chunks of rock and earth. Agriculture is restricted by a lack of flatlands and ground water, but the Virgins' potential as a playground is great; they have fine beaches and breath-taking vistas; from the deck of a vessel cruising the Sir Francis Drake Channel, the profusion of islands sometimes obscures the sight of the sea, giving the feeling of a huge, blue-green lake. Roughly 500 miles across the open Atlantic to the northwest and outside the Caribbean archipelago lie the far more prosperous, equally beautiful British Bahamas, whose coral sands and modern pleasure domes attract some 300,000 tourists each year.

Since colonial times the British islands have been more aware of the width—and the occasional hostility—of the channels that divide them than of their narrowness. Yet the channels are in fact narrow. Barbados and Jamaica are the only British islands that lie completely out of sight of one or more of the others; in the normal course of travel, Grenada is not visible from Trinidad at deck level, but it looms ahead before the peaks of Trinidad disappear astern. Most transportation between islands has been by wind or hand power—in crude native sloops and schooners or cranky fishing dugouts. Communications are, however, better than they were a generation ago, when a letter from Jamaica to the eastern islands had to be routed through New York, London or Halifax. Today the Trinidadian-owned airline island-hops daily. Between islands too small for the turboprops and jets to land, light planes flit, and there is a constant population flow back and forth.

AMONG islanders who left home, a recent Barbadian carnival queen was from St. Vincent; some of the pan-beaters in an Antiguan steel band are from St. Kitts; a tourist aide in St. Lucia is Grenadian; and workers in the giant oil refineries of Curaçao and Aruba come from all over the Caribbean. The destination of thousands of foot-loose West Indians is Trinidad, richest of all the islands and itself a complex racial pepper pot.

Trinidad's population is so mixed that no group can claim a clear majority. Negroes account for perhaps 40 per cent. Descendants of slaves and Europeans number some 15 per cent. Chinese account for about 1 per cent and descendants of immigrants from India—known in the islands as "East Indians"—for about 35 per cent. Europeans account for less than 2 per cent. There are antagonisms among these groups, but forced coexistence has enabled the Trinidadian to develop a devil-may-care individuality that is unique; it allows him to live as he pleases and to laugh at people who do not dare do the same, and to laugh even at himself so long as the joke has wit and bite.

Trinidad is the southernmost of the West Indies, separated from South America only by two narrow channels called Dragon's Mouths and Serpent's Mouth. Often the sun rises into a dazzlingly clear sky over Port of Spain, and in the residential areas that are pushing up the wooded hillsides behind the city, the shrill cries of tropical birds compete with crowing cocks. The city itself is as heterogeneous as any colonial port, crowding new construction of reinforced concrete against Victorian wood. Shady Woodford Square rings to the voices of soapbox orators. A mile away Queen's Park Savannah is fringed by fantasy—the turreted and

voluted mansions of another day—overlooked by the glassy stare of the Hilton Hotel. A few miles in the other direction a large, filthy shantytown, diminishing through government action, is guarded by wheeling turkey vultures.

Trinidad is smaller and is potentially less wealthy than Puerto Rico, and its early history is largely one of neglect. The colonizing Spanish, who were there from 1498 to 1797, could not supply the manpower to operate it successfully as an agricultural colony. Spain insisted on the usual trade monopoly but failed to implement it; one governor complained that no Spanish ship had arrived for 20 years. Almost every commercial transaction was therefore illegal, and the foundations for anarchy were laid. In 1783, Spain faced the facts and opened Trinidad to colonization by a strictly defined type of foreigner: a Roman Catholic subject of a nation in alliance with Spain. Land grants and tax exemptions—favorite incentives still—were offered to sweeten the invitation, and Frenchmen, most of them in flight from Haiti or from the French Revolution, arrived with their slaves in large numbers. In 1797 a British fleet descended on Port of Spain, and the tiny Spanish garrison surrendered without firing a shot; Trinidad, already more French than Spanish, became nominally British.

SLAVERY came to an end in the British islands in 1834, before it was able to dominate the patterns of Trinidadian society; most of the Negro population scattered as soon as possible into the hills to scrape a living from the land. The search for a new labor supply that would cost no more than slaves added another ingredient to the pepper pot. The British government subsidized the importation of laborers from overseas. They were indentured to the planters for five years and then, if they lived that long, granted either land in Trinidad or passage home. Few of the Portuguese and Chinese who tried it could withstand the combination of climate, filth and disease, but the East Indians were more adaptable. As many as 3,000 a year arrived until 1917, when India put a stop to the system. Planters often treated them even worse than they had the slaves, and the sight provided a kind of ironic satisfaction to the Negroes. Nevertheless, the East Indians increased and settled in the southern parts of the island, and eventually they challenged the political domination of the Negroes.

BARRACKS life without sanitation or privacy was the rule for the workers in both city and country in the mid-19th Century, encouraging a kind of community lawlessness that the government failed to recognize for what it really was: a symptom of mounting discontent and frustration. Instead of correcting the causes of the trouble, the government ordered police into action on several memorable occasions: the famous *canboulay* riots during the carnival seasons of 1881, 1882 and 1883 were paralleled by the less publicized uprising of East Indians during their Hosein festival in 1884. In 1903 the Water Riots took place, in which one of the issues was, in all seriousness, the compulsory installation of water meters. The riots of 1937 began when police tried to arrest a popular speaker at a workers' rally, and they turned grim when a policeman was burned alive.

This time the violence had the effect of uniting the island's working people in a practical labor movement which eventually resulted in political awareness. Earlier, oil had been discovered, and by 1909 it was being produced in commercial quantities. Trinidad became the richest of the West Indies. Its per capita income rose to $580 in 1961, and its rate of growth has averaged an impressive 8.5 per cent in recent years. Negroes and mulattoes were still in the majority when Crown Colony status was lifted in 1956, and they proceeded to elect the brilliant, peppery Eric Williams, an Oxford graduate and history scholar, as the island's chief minister.

Under Williams' administration, Trinidad became an independent member of the British Commonwealth of Nations in 1962, but only after a turbulent interlude during which it became the proposed capital of the Federation of the West Indies. Well before the end of the 19th Century, various royal commissions had investigated the possibility of federation between the islands, but nothing permanent had resulted. Nevertheless, the idea was pursued as the years passed, and finally, in 1956, a constitution acceptable to all—because it bound them to practically nothing—was signed. Trinidad and Jamaica, the richest and biggest, stood to lose most but seemed to have accepted the inevitable, and in 1958 the Federation of the West Indies came into nominal existence. Then, on the very eve of the federation's being granted independence four years later, Jamaica chose to remove itself from the group.

Jamaica had always been unenthusiastic about federation. The island lies 1,000 miles to the west of the other British islands; it has large deposits of bauxite (the raw material of aluminum); and it has a recent history of successful, if limited, industrialization. Its awesomely steep mountains and pretty beaches make it a natural center for that other modern industry, tourism. Its population is not only the largest but also the least stable in the British islands, being moody and sometimes ungovernable.

DISORDERS were frequent both before and after emancipation in Jamaica. The number of runaway slaves was high, for the penalties for flight, terrible as they were, were no worse than those that befell slaves in everyday life. Three years before emancipation actually took place in 1834, the slaves were inflamed by the idea that they had already been freed but that the news was being withheld. Fields were burned, houses destroyed and planters attacked—and afterward hundreds of slaves were executed. Once free, most of the 250,000 ex-slaves dispersed to the hills. Coincidentally, the British government at home, abandoning long-standing protectionist trade policies, cut import duties on sugar grown in non-British territories. Unable to compete, the Jamaican economy disintegrated. Plantations were abandoned, and cholera and yellow fever swept through the populace. Inevitably, crime increased. In 1865 a gathering in the town of Morant Bay became a riot; white men were killed, the militia was called out, and the punishment was swift and brutal. Crown Colony rule was imposed, and the island continued in that undignified status until 1944.

Most remarkable of the many personalities who influenced Jamaica before World War I was the magnetic Marcus Garvey. Born in Jamaica in 1887, he went to the United States in 1916 and during the 1920s drew considerable attention; his Universal Negro Improvement Association aroused alarm, for it preached Negro superiority. Garvey was eventually deported to Jamaica after serving two years of a five-year term for mail fraud. He is quoted as saying "look to Africa, when a black king will be crowned, for the day of deliverance is near." He inspired many thousands with his preachments that God was black, that Negroes had once ruled the world and, most significantly, that Africa was their destiny.

Partly out of his teachings came an unusual Jamaican politico-religious cult, the Ras Tafari movement. It is named for Ras Tafari, who became Emperor Haile Selassie of Ethiopia in 1930, an event that was interpreted as fulfillment of Garvey's prophecy. Ras Tafarian dogma is as involuted as the *vodou* spirit world, but in general it posits that Ras Tafari is the living God, that Negroes are the chosen race, and Africa is the Promised Land. White men are the Babylonian oppressors. The personal habits of many Ras Tafarians are antisocial; they refuse to wash their bodies or cut their hair, and they dress in filthy rags. They make their headquarters in the teeming slums of Kingston, where there may be 20,000 of them.

SOCIAL consciousness among the working classes of Jamaica was catalyzed in 1938 when the workers were organized into a labor union by a colorful leader named Alexander Bustamante. In those days Bustamante was described as a firebrand, and the agitation he caused landed him in jail several times. He was extracted by his cousin, Norman Washington Manley, a distinguished lawyer who carried Bustamante's work a step further and organized the workers into the People's National party. Although they were for many years associates in the labor movement, Bustamante and Manley eventually became political rivals.

MANLEY was prime minister in 1962. He had been in favor of federation, but he made the mistake of staging a plebiscite on the issue, apparently expecting it to be simply a vote of confidence. The outside world saw no reason to doubt the smooth progress of events; publications spoke of an independent federation as an accomplished fact. But Bustamante was opposed to federation, and his old magic —and his dire warnings that the island and its economy would be dragged down by poorer neighbors—upset the vote. Jamaica was obliged to withdraw. In a subsequent election Bustamante replaced Manley as prime minister, and Jamaica opted to become an independent member of the British Commonwealth.

The dénouement was swift. Trinidad, which had agreed to the weak confederation only because Jamaica was in it, also declared for independence. Britain agreed, apparently without reluctance, to both petitions. Bustamante, as prime minister of the new Jamaican nation, immediately pledged his friendship to the U.S., while Trinidad's Premier Eric Williams pointedly had nothing friendly to say.

Predictably, both new nations suffered a slump following their independence, but both economies later began an upward trend. Jamaica's industrialization program is producing its greatest income, but bauxite mining, bananas and tourism are important contributors. Trinidad's oil fields continue to provide its most important source of income.

Oil was also discovered under Barbados, and that tiny island planned to become independent in late 1966. This move, along with Antigua's, left the remaining "Little Seven" British islands a choice of facing up to modern economic realities or foundering in their own selfish and antique methods.

Under a banner of his political party, Eric Williams, the prime minister of Trinidad and Tobago, addresses an evening rally.

New Nations Busily Exercising Their Freedom

Granted independence by Britain in 1962, the young nations of Jamaica and Trinidad and Tobago are engaged in improving already viable economies and in learning the intricacies of self-government. While the legislative process may have a distinctive local flavor, democracy functions well. Industry, encouraged by Britain, continues to grow, making the islands less dependent on sugar and other crops. Indeed, traces of Britain's long rule are everywhere, set handsomely if unexpectedly against a background of tropical forest and southern sea.

DEMOCRATIC RULE in Jamaica
is closely modeled on the
parliamentary system of Great Britain

HOUSE SESSION is presided over by the bewigged Speaker, Tacius Golding *(above)*, whose authority in Jamaica's House of Representatives is symbolized by the sterling silver mace, a close copy of the one always present in Britain's House of Commons.

CABINET MEETING is led by white-haired Sir Alexander Bustamante, prime minister and one of those most active in securing Jamaican independence in 1962. As in Britain, the Cabinet is composed of members of the legislature's majority party.

CRICKET BOWLER flings the ball on a hedge-enclosed field as a batsman in pads awaits his turn. Jamaicans are enthusiastic cricketers and some rank among the world's best players.

YOUNG CHURCHGOERS tarry by a blossoming bush *(right)* on their way to a small Roman Catholic church in a village near Kingston. The constitution guarantees freedom of religion.

BUSY TRINIDAD, *with valuable oil deposits and several important crops, seems*

destined for a prosperous future

TRACK MEET between several of the 27 public schools in populous and energetic Port of Spain draws athletes and spectators to the handsome "Oval" of the Queens Park Cricket Club.

HELMETED WORKER cycles home from the big Texaco oil refinery *(left)* in Pointe-à-Pierre which yields 275,000 barrels a day. Oil provides more than 80 per cent of Trinidad's exports.

COCONUT PALMS filter the afternoon sun as a harvester with a donkey cart picks up fallen coconuts. Oil from coconut meat is used in soapmaking, a thriving small industry in Trinidad.

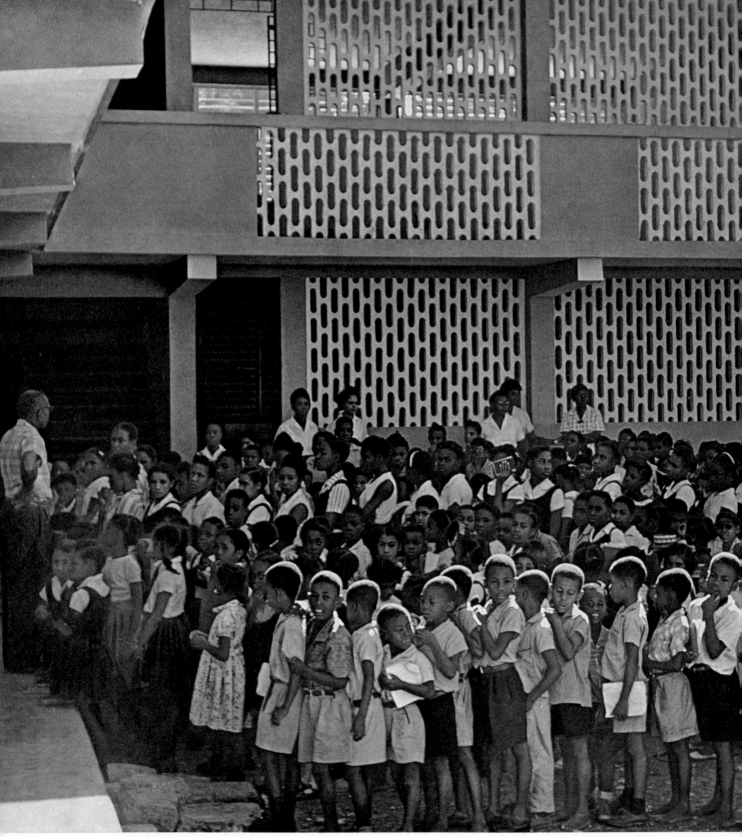

CONTEMPORARY SCHOOL with cement grillwork walls for light and air is a by-product of Jamaica's drive, encouraged by Prime Minister Bustamante, to increase and improve schooling.

MEDICAL STUDENT concentrates in the stacks of the library at the University of the West Indies outside Kingston. The university is open to all qualified English-speaking students.

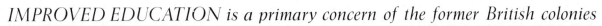
IMPROVED EDUCATION is a primary concern of the former British colonies

State-supported children in uniform, who live together in an expropriated Havana country club to study Marxism and fine arts as part of

the Castro program in Cuba, practice military drill on the terrace.

8

Out of a Spanish Mold

THE North American who is thrown into contact with residents of the Caribbean may find the West Indian of Hispanic origin the most difficult to understand. To the North American, the "Latin" seems to possess a tendency to sudden violence over what seems little provocation. His loves seem tempestuous, his hatreds implacable. It is indisputable that time means something different to him: punctuality is not necessarily a virtue (it may indicate too much emphasis on trivia). His is a small world, and he feels most comfortable when he is very close to or even touching another person— the social scientist Edward T. Hall says that many a North American has unconsciously snubbed a Latin by insisting on maintaining a distance of about two feet in conversation.

A marked spontaneity pervades much of Latin life: for the worker who traditionally lives from harvest to harvest, planning ahead is of little use; nevertheless, the Hispano-American forms friendships slowly and keeps them until

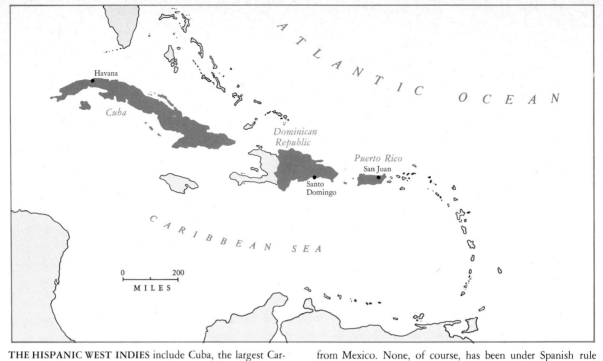

THE HISPANIC WEST INDIES include Cuba, the largest Caribbean island; the Dominican Republic; and Puerto Rico. All lie along the route of Spanish treasure fleets which sailed to and from Mexico. None, of course, has been under Spanish rule since 1898, but in all three Spanish is the principal language and something much like the Spanish temperament persists.

death; they are the foundation of his business as well as of his social life. He is, however, impulsive and quick in his warmheartedness toward his fellow man.

The Latin West Indian holds a wholehearted belief in man, and particularly in two basic human qualities: *machismo,* or virility, and *dignidad,* or self-respect. The value he places on *dignidad* accounts, more than any sense of constitutional rights, for his love of freedom, which is as genuine and abiding as that of anyone in the world, and he is quite honestly willing to die for it. He is thus a formidable revolutionist, and sometimes an explosive human being. He may be offended, or feel degraded, restrained or pressured by matters that are elsewhere accepted as normal. He will not, for example, accept a favor unless he is in a position to reciprocate immediately. One manifestation of this cross-cultural conflict is his incomprehensible—to some Americans—resentment of the United States.

In the day-to-day life of the laborer, *machismo* takes the form of achieving, or at least claiming, excellence in sports, fighting or even in cutting cane—and most of all in *amor.* The *macho* hopes to beget as many boy-children as possible (begetting girls apparently indicates a slightly lower order of virility). The *macho* may be a poet or an artist but he is, as a rule, an active rather than a reflective man; if he chooses to express the greatness of his soul through words, he often declaims poetry or orates; Fidel Castro's five-hour television speeches are as admired for their heroic proportions as for their messages.

THE idea of *machismo* is also related to the history of oppression that has been the political lot of Cuba and the Dominican Republic. When the individual Cuban or Dominican has been unable fully to express his *machismo* in his personal life, he has often transferred it to a public figure who displays the necessary greatness of spirit, sometimes a poet or a sports hero, but more likely a colorful military or political leader—a Gerardo Machado, a Fulgencio Batista, a Rafael Trujillo or a Fidel Castro. He places great trust in his public heroes, even though he can probably remember the disillusionment he eventually came to feel about the previous demagogue.

The early histories of the Hispanic colonies of Cuba, Santo Domingo and Puerto Rico were similar. Each fortified its best harbor to shelter the great Spanish treasure fleets as they painfully beat their way upwind from Mexico. When the colonies' meager veins of gold were worked out, all three gradually tamed their flatlands, shifting in the process from herding to agriculture. As they produced exportable products, and as their own needs for imports increased, they developed talents for smuggling to avoid Spain's restrictive trade monopoly. Then in 1762 the histories began to diverge: while the easterly pair for the time being carried on undisturbed by troublesome contact with foreigners, Cuba was invaded and occupied for 10 months by the British; the effect was to give Cubans a glimpse of new commercial opportunities. Not long afterward, Santo Domingo began to lose its early eminence and to take the position it was to hold past the mid-20th Century, that of a rather introverted Caribbean capital. Little Puerto Rico was relegated to the position of an outpost.

Havana, however, turned its face outward and began its career as one of the world's cosmopolitan cities—as befitted the capital of such a large and increasingly wealthy colony. Its society was further broadened in the early 19th Century by the arrival of refugees from revolutions in Haiti and South America and by immigrants from Europe. Soon the city contained a number of scholarly and professional societies for the exchange of information, much of it of the fashionable European liberal flavor. Books and periodicals circulated freely, and Spain's promises of representation in the home country's legislature inspired the Cuban liberals with hope for further improvements in Spanish colonial policy.

CUBA'S progress toward political maturity was interrupted by a policy reversal in Spain. Increasing restrictions on Cuban trade were imposed; the colonial administration became more and more despotic over the next half century. During this time, fulminations of various Cuban exile groups in New York and Florida against Spanish colonial policies aroused traditional American sympathy for the underdog. Moreover, the United States resented the presence of a European power off its own coast. As the Cuban leader José Martí began the final revolution in 1895, the terrible repressive measures imposed upon the Cuban people by the Spanish General Valeriano ("The Butcher") Weyler united the populations of the United States and Cuba alike. After the U.S.S. *Maine* was sunk by a mysterious explosion in Havana harbor in 1898, the yellow, jingoist press stirred up passions in the U.S., and the United States declared war on Spain.

CUBAN revolutionaries were not overjoyed to see the U.S. entering their fight. They were still less pleased after the defeat of Spain when they learned the terms of America's Platt Amendment, accepted by the new Cuban government and made a part of the country's constitution—which was drawn up under American supervision in 1901. The amendment asserted the right of the United States to intervene if Cuban independence or Cuban "life, property and individual liberty" were threatened, and to establish naval bases on Cuban soil—the provision that accounts for the existence of the controversial Guantánamo Bay base.

Between the evacuation of U.S. forces in 1902 and the victory of Castro's revolution in 1959, Cuba's politics were so chaotic that the Americans felt compelled to intervene time and again to restore order, sometimes by sending Marines, sometimes by sending "advisers," sometimes by dispatching stiff diplomatic warnings. The constitution was observed only haphazardly; when it was not entirely ignored, the strong men simply evaded its provisions. Still, there was prosperity for some. After World War I, sugar rose from five cents to more than 22 cents a pound; the financial juggling became known as the Dance of the Millions, and Havana became a gaudy, sinful playground for the very rich.

In 1920, the bubble burst, sugar dropped below four cents, millionaires became paupers and Gerardo Machado, who became one of Cuba's most ruthless strong men, assumed power. Machado was forced into exile in 1933, despite the fact that he had closed the centers of opposition—the high schools and the university—and deported or destroyed scores of his opponents. Out of that holocaust rose Fulgencio Batista, a sergeant who with a cadre of other noncommissioned officers ejected the regular officers, took control of the army and seized control of the state.

Batista's method was, at first, to rule through obedient presidents (one disobedient one was impeached) while he called himself chief of staff. Later, in 1940, he was elected president by a large and apparently enthusiastic majority, although he fell into disfavor before the 1944 election, which his puppet candidate lost. For several years he remained in the background, but in 1952 Batista again resorted to force and became dictator, dissolving congress and suppressing all political parties. Despite the lack of freedom, the period was one of prosperity for planters and industrialists (including a large number of Americans). In 1954, apparently feeling the need to legitimize his position, Batista staged an election against a phantom opposition, and then, in an expansive mood, freed hundreds of political prisoners—including a young revolutionary named Fidel Castro.

To the working classes of Cuba—as to the same groups at the same time in the Dominican Republic—the various strong men who ruled were not entirely oppressors. In a sense, they were idealized *machos*. They were victors in the treacherous and intricate field of traditional Latin American politics, where rules are fluid as rain and where the ultimate result is almost certainly violent death or exile; they

---

HISPANIOLA, THE DIVIDED ISLAND

The island which today includes Haiti and the Dominican Republic was originally called La Isla Española—the Spanish Island—by Columbus. Its principal settlement was Santo Domingo. By 1700 the settlement's name was being applied throughout the island: the Spanish called their part Santo Domingo and the French called their part Saint-Domingue. Meanwhile, the island as a whole came to be known by the Latinized version of the original name, Hispaniola. When the French half became independent in 1804 it adopted the name Haiti, the aboriginal word for "mountainous country." In 1844 the Spanish half began calling itself the Dominican Republic.

---

lived lives of splendor, as befitted heroes. The leaders were so deeply identified with their positions that the "movements" took their names: *trujillismo, machadismo, batistismo* and, in a significant turn toward intimacy, *fidelismo*, rather than *castrismo*. This psychological habit has inevitably contributed to the long-standing emphasis on personalism in government, out of which has come so much plundering of the economies of the Hispanic islands, so much bloodshed and so much contempt for politics and for government itself.

Fidel Castro has been the most nearly ideal hero to appear in Cuba in modern times. He was born on his father's sugar plantation on August 13, 1926, in Oriente province, the cradle of Cuban revolutionary activity. His radical, anti-imperialist, anticapitalist tendencies were born in the 1940s when he was a student at the University of Havana. Castro combines physical bigness, strength and athleticism with a reputation for intellect and a formidable gift for oratory. He projects his role as a man of the people by affecting coarse military clothes, a gross beard and a cigar; he awes his followers with messianic claims, saying that it was the force of history rather than personal ambition that cast him as leader. Many of his five-hour speeches, while seemingly discursive, are actually well organized. Even when he was a young radical, his enemies recognized the power of his oratory: his trial after his effort to launch a revolution by an attack on the Moncada army barracks on July 26, 1953, was held behind closed doors. When he was granted freedom in Batista's amnesty of 1955, the government forbade him to speak on the radio.

After his release, Castro spent a year and a half in Mexico, preparing his next move. He obtained money from Cuban exiles in New York and Florida, trained a military cadre, and maintained contacts with revolutionaries at home in Cuba. His invasion took place on an Oriente beach on December 2, 1956—two days behind schedule. It was a disaster. Castro's men were hit by government troops almost immediately after landing; of the 82 invaders, only Castro and 11 others escaped to reach the Sierra Maestra mountains.

AFTER this setback, the world believed Castro to be dead until Herbert L. Matthews of *The New York Times* made a daring journey to Castro's hide-out in the remote Sierra Maestra in 1957 and wrote a series of friendly articles about the bearded, dedicated revolutionary and his guerrilla followers. Other journalists followed; some had reservations about him, but Castro rapidly became established in the public eye. Meanwhile, Batista intensified his oppression and the insurrection gained popularity thereby. The early history of Castro's take-over in January of 1959 is familiar: the vengeance-killing of Batista's bullies in Havana, the quick restoration of order, Castro's triumphal march to the capital, the accumulation of support from dissident revolutionary movements, the swift execution of "traitors," and the joy of Cubans at the success of the revolution. Even when it became apparent that Castro was drifting toward another one-man government, he retained the loyalty of the Cuban masses.

Disillusionment began when Fidel the reformer took over Fidel the revolutionary. Castro remained vague about the policies of the revolution and yet demanded unswerving support as he announced contradictory decisions. His followers discovered that he was addicted to flattery; he threw tantrums when he was criticized, and criticism soon became perilous. Gradually many of his longtime supporters, some of them Cuba's most experienced administrators, were dismissed, denounced or demoted, and eventually they were forced to leave the island.

One difference between Castro and his predecessors was the content of his promises. While Machado and Batista said that they wished to set things in order so that the old system could function to the eventual benefit of all Cubans, Castro proposed to establish a utopia, a state of perfection.

At the beginning of his revolution, there were those who thought—and there are those who still think—that at the time Castro was idealist enough to mean what he said, and he was in fact the only strong man in Cuban history strong enough to attempt large-scale reform. But, like many another revolutionary, the only way he could think of to start his country on the road to perfection was to attempt to transfer to the people the power and prerogatives once limited to owners of property. Large estates were broken up, and the land thus gained was redistributed to the peasants. The "vital minimum," Castro declared, was 66 acres for a family of five. In addition, a housing program was launched and a literacy campaign begun. Initially, food production increased, and in the first surge of enthusiasm for the revolution, Castro's promises of new schools and housing were at least partially fulfilled. But inexperience and mismanagement resulted in unforeseen shortages and delays; Cubans who formerly endured hunger because they believed it was their lot could not stand the same hunger when food had been promised. Castro showed his growing concern by his repeated warnings that everybody would have to make sacrifices before utopia could be attained.

AT the outset Castro insisted that his program had nothing to do with Soviet Communism. Very possibly, it did not. In May 1959 he was still criticizing Communism because it suppressed liberties (and capitalism because it "starves people"). The danger lay in the fact that Castro was in a position to try practically anything he wanted, and if his original supporters did not wish to continue the revolution under his leadership, he could find others who did—among the country's hard core of young radicals.

As important as Castro's rather naive idealism was his deep mistrust of the United States. Along with most educated Cubans, he resented the presence of U.S. fighting forces on Cuban soil and the prominence of powerful American corporations among Cuba's most important property holders. Ideologically, he felt that the U.S. represented powerful conservative pressures. When Washington shortsightedly failed to give him what he thought was proper recognition, he turned on the U.S. and took over American property, straining already taut international relations. Since the local Communist party was already deeply involved with his revolution, it was only natural for Castro to turn to Soviet Russia as he turned from the United States—and as the United States turned from him.

AFTER that the Castro revolution was grim. The army again exercised power in political affairs, and a greatly expanded civil militia became a major prop of government. Together, the army and the militia indoctrinated civilians and formed the base of a universal person-to-person spy system that handily revealed the slightest anti-Castro deviation. To make control easier, periodicals and broadcasting stations, professional societies and public institutions of learning—all the traditional nests of opposition, as Castro well knew from his own revolutionary days—were taken over or infiltrated by Castro supporters. To make matters grimmer, Russia coolly picked up her missiles and departed after the U.S. ultimatum of 1963, and Russo-Cuban relations were never the same again. Castro apparently suffered disillusionment again when he tried later to establish a profitable relationship with Red China.

Ironically, Cuban exiles seemed to be doing everything in their power to further the Castro revolution, each new move from outside either fulfilling a Castro prediction or providing him with material for propaganda. The irresponsible raids by exiles in armed pleasure boats were only ant bites, but Castro magnified them to scorpion stings, charging that the raiders were supported by the U.S. He pointed to the Bay of Pigs invasion of 1961 as confirmation of his warnings about the intentions of the United States, and, as additional evidence of American hostility, asserted that the U.S. was sheltering *batistianos*. At any rate, by 1966 Cuban exiles had lost much of their militancy.

At home, despite administrative mistakes, supply shortages and jails full of political prisoners, Fidel was as strong as ever—a fact that is easier to understand when it is realized that more Cubans owned more property and felt more certain that their needs were heeded than ever before.

Across the narrow windward passage, in the Dominican Republic, a situation arose in 1962 which seemed geared for the expansion of Castro Communism. The dictator Rafael Trujillo had been assassinated in May 1961, and the republic had sunk into the kind of aimless turbulence that is characteristic of so much of Latin American politics. Briefly, Trujillo's son Ramfis and Trujillo's tame president, Joaquín Balaguer, assumed power; unable to obtain popular support, both were shortly forced into exile. The situation was obviously ideal for a well-organized Communist movement. Cuban Castroites funneled unknown sums into the Dominican Republic. Leftist groups fostered riots and minor disorders, but the chaos failed to become general. When elections were finally held in December 1962, most of the eligible voters went to the polls. The winner of the presidential race was Juan Bosch; his victory appeared honest and democratic.

THE Dominican Republic had been in a most unlikely position to show much command of applied democracy. For the preceding 31 years—a lifetime for most of its people—the nation had known only the stultifying dictatorship of Trujillo. Even before the Trujillo era, there had been little to give Dominicans much confidence in government. On the eve of declaring its independence from Spain early in the 19th Century, the nation was seized by Haiti; not until 1844 did it attain freedom. Constantly in fear of a re-establishment of Haitian control, and unable to organize a workable government of their own, Dominicans spent most of the subsequent years trying to place themselves under the rule of a foreign power. In 1861, after being rejected by France, Britain and the United States, they actually restored themselves to Spanish colonial status for four disastrous years. American military rule was imposed on them between 1916 and 1924 after the island's economy and politics had been reduced to near-chaos. The occupation had a more salubrious effect on the economy than on the Dominicans' self-esteem, and it had an unforeseen side effect. While there, the Americans put the National Guard on a businesslike footing. Among the trainees was young Rafael Trujillo. When revolt broke out in 1930, Trujillo, by then army chief of staff, seized power.

IT is not unusual to hear in post-Trujillo Santo Domingo that the dictator was not so bad. Some Dominicans point out improvements that Trujillo made: extensive irrigation projects, new water systems in the cities and improved roads. Trujillo also constructed new schools, nationalized the power and telephone services, beautified the capital and improved public-health services. It is not easy for Dominicans to realize that these improvements, like the 2,000-odd statues of himself erected around the countryside, were created by "El Benefactor" largely to improve his own image in the eyes of the world. The irrigation system is inadequate. The school-building project raised the literacy rate only to some 30 per cent. Prosperity was limited to members of the upper class, while vast numbers of Dominicans were homeless, jobless and close to starvation. The Dominican reply to this is that conditions are even worse over the hills in Haiti—an indisputable, if irrelevant, fact.

Even after Bosch was elected, many Dominicans remained reluctant to discuss the negative aspects of *trujillismo* except to point out,

THE NETHERLANDS ANTILLES

Permanently assigned to the Dutch at the end of the Napoleonic Wars, which decided the disposition of so many of the Spanish discoveries, the Netherlands Antilles consist of two groups of islands, separated by some 550 miles of sea. Off the South American coast lie Curaçao, Aruba and Bonaire, which the Dutch call the Leewards. In the northeastern Caribbean are the Dutch Windwards —Sint Maarten, Sint Eustatius and Saba.

THE WINDWARDS

The beauty of the three northeastern islands is gradually making them prime tourist attractions, but apart from this they have little economic importance. Sint Maarten raises horses and mules for export. Saba, an extinct volcano rising sheer from the sea, produces little but lace. Sint Eustatius (Statia) earns only a precarious living from small farms and the sea.

THE LEEWARDS

Once an important source of salt, Bonaire today produces little of commercial value, but it is rich in bird life, its marshes alive with flamingos. Far more prosperous are Curaçao and Aruba, important oil-refining centers.

GOVERNMENT

Granted complete autonomy in their internal affairs after World War II, the islands are now integral parts of the Kingdom of the Netherlands, reigned over by the Dutch royal house, and constitutionally equal to Holland itself.

without much factual evidence, that the early days of the dictatorship were not days of terror, but only of mounting apprehension caused by increasing surveillance. Yet as much as two years after Trujillo's assassination, habits of a lifetime continued to give a furtive air to Santo Domingo. Downtown streets in the capital were nearly deserted except at rush hours. Even in the safety of their homes at night, Dominicans hesitated in midsentence at the sound of a Volkswagen engine, remembering former nights when they had stopped breathing until the sound of the VW security-police car had passed their houses, never knowing who was about to be summarily arrested and tortured. Some peasant families, on the other hand, enjoyed the transition period, squatting in the various Trujillo family mansions about the country after stripping them of their furniture, toilets, sinks and even panes of glass.

The tragedy of the Dominican Republic was that Trujillo very nearly broke the human spirit of the more than three million Dominicans. It is hard to imagine just what he thought of the people he ruled. Toward the end, when he was beginning to suspect even his close associates, he treated everybody very much as the colonial landowners had treated slaves, as creatures who were expected to serve him or give him pleasure—or die for failure to do so.

TRUJILLO tried extremely hard to manipulate North Americans. He attempted to woo high-ranking molders of American public opinion by inviting them to Santo Domingo and lavishing hospitality on them. At his invitation, the Brooklyn Dodgers once did their spring training on the island. It was said that he promoted the Dominican *merengue* in U.S. dance studios as a public-relations gesture. To preserve his public image, he went so far as to kidnap Jesús de Galíndez, a scholar who disappeared in New York in 1956 just as his doctoral dissertation on the corruption of the Trujillo regime was about to be published. When Trujillo's reputation seemed to be getting tarnished, he set himself up as the hemisphere's staunchest Red-hater. At home, where the economy was feeling the effect of sanctions imposed by the Organization of American States, even once-staunch *trujillistas* lost faith. The end might have been anticipated. Despite his elaborate precautions, "El Benefactor" was ambushed on a country road in 1961.

In the Dominican Republic, as in Cuba, the eradication of a tyrant is celebrated by a flaring of hope—which always, so far, has been quickly betrayed by a new leader. No new leader has yet had a chance to consolidate his position in the post-Trujillo Dominican Republic. The interim government, which took over in January 1962, did not attempt to perpetuate itself in power, or to install its own man in the presidency or to de-Trujillize the country—although it did remove the obvious fanatics from positions of power. It proceeded instead to prepare the electorate for a democratic election with such success that, in spite of the attempts of the Communists to disrupt the procedure,

1.1 million out of 1.6 million eligible Dominicans voted.

Like the leaders of the interim regime, Bosch realized that after three decades under Trujillo, almost everybody in the country might be tainted by *trujillismo*, and he promised to avoid a purge. Equally important to the mass of voters was his promise to distribute land among the peasants, including vast acres once held by members of the assassinated dictator's family. His victory was a landslide.

On the face of it, there were thus grounds for hope in the Dominican Republic. It is a relatively vast and fertile land. Among its considerable natural resources are the rather courtly friendliness and good looks of its people, and the grandeur of its interior scenery, which should be sufficient to attract a profitable flow of tourists. But the economy that Bosch took over stood close to ruin. An estimated $800 million in assets was held outside the country by the Trujillo clan. The great sugar and coffee plantations remained in desperate need of experienced operators and laborers.

ALTHOUGH at the time of his inauguration Bosch appeared confident of solving his problems, the business community remained wary. He stayed in office for a bare seven months before the army, still residually *trujillista*, forced him into exile. In April 1965 junior officers attempted to restore Bosch. In the bloody fighting that ensued, U.S. troops intervened, and were augmented by contingents sent by five other members of the Organization of American States. There was a period of pacification, punctuated by bloodshed. Then an election in June 1966 returned to office an old Trujillo collaborator, philosopher-poet Joaquín Balaguer, who had been the last president under Trujillo.

The people were tired; they wanted peace even at the price of needed change. But the nation's problems were still unsolved—the principal problem being how to get the army out of politics so that the Dominican Republic could finally develop normal democratic institutions.

Fidel Castro holds a vast Cuban crowd enthralled with his voice, a weapon more crucial to his regime's survival than Soviet arms.

A Tragic Penchant for Dictators and Strong Men

The Spanish-speaking islands of the West Indies, with the exception of Puerto Rico, have a modern, as well as an ancient, history of political unrest, dictatorial rule and bloodshed. One of the worst of the despots was Rafael Trujillo, dictator of the Dominican Republic for 31 years and the master of a terrorist secret police. Trujillo and his relatives had grabbed one third of the country's land and many of its businesses before an assassin's machine gun ended his rule in 1961. The liberated Dominican Republic has proved difficult to govern, for the country was left with an explosive backlog of inequities and tensions. Cuba has an even more tragic history, having traded a ruthless dictator, Batista, for a Communist strong man, Castro.

MAN ON HORSEBACK, Trujillo enjoys a weekend ride on his country estate. In his 31 years as dictator of the Dominican Republic, Trujillo was responsible for an estimated 25,000 deaths.

MOURNING WOMEN *(right),* whose husbands disappeared in Trujillo's prisons, demonstrate in December 1961 against President Balaguer, a holdover from the dictatorship. He soon quit.

JOYFUL YOUTHS *(below)* celebrate the defeat of an attempt by Trujillo's family to retake power six months after his death. The struggle against *trujillistas* still goes on, much muted.

the cruel dictatorship of Rafael Trujillo

SUSPECTED SPY believed to have been a Trujillo police agent is beaten by a mob on a Santo Domingo street. Trujillo's police spies sent a stream of victims to his two torture chambers.

ARMED REBELS (*below*), who tried in 1965 to restore democratically elected Juan Bosch to the presidency from which the army had ousted him, stride through downtown Santo Domingo.

AMERICAN TANKS patrol a corridor cut between the Dominican army and rebels to halt fighting that began in April 1965. The U.S. moved in within four days, and five Latin American powers later sent troops. Although the U.S. contingent numbered 21,000 of the 23,000-man force, a Brazilian commanded. Washington wanted this; its intervention had drawn heavy criticism.

JUAN BOSCH (*above*) declaims to supporters upon his return from exile in Puerto Rico, where he had gone in 1963 after being ousted from the presidency. In 1966 he ran for office again.

JOAQUIN BALAGUER, who first held the presidency under Trujillo, campaigns against Bosch in 1966. In the election he won an overwhelming mandate from the war-weary Dominican people.

STRONGMAN Fulgencio Batista, who seized power in a 1952 coup, addresses the Cuban people. He relied on the army which kept him in power to put down the rebel Castro. But Castro had only to wait until the regime collapsed of its own corruption and ineptitude.

REBEL Fidel Castro strikes a heroic pose at his hideout in the mountains. The important actions of the revolution occurred not here, where Castro is shown with his brother Raúl *(kneeling, center)* and other camp-mates, but in the cities where faceless partisans committed sabotage.

and "Fidel" emerged as a national hero

FLAG-WAVING LIBERATORS, members of the triumphant Castro forces, arrive to throw open Havana Prison on February 1, 1959, the morning after Batista fled. At top, political prisoners of the Batista regime watch from the wall of the old fortress.

123

CASTRO'S BETRAYAL of
Cuban hopes for a democracy
became clear as he assumed
the role of a demagogue

BEARDED STRONG MAN talks to his aides dressed in fatigues such as he wore in the mountains. After victory he kept beard and uniform as a reminder that his revolution was unfinished.

TELEVISION SPEECH by Castro *(opposite)* on January 9, 1959, the day after he entered Havana, was the first of many such harangues. Castro has often given speeches lasting four hours.

GIGANTIC MURAL in which "Fidel" looks like a Biblical prophet dominates a crowd waiting to hear Castro on May Day, 1962. The sign contains an excerpt from one of his previous speeches.

PORQUE ESTA GRAN
HUMANIDAD HA DICHO
¡BASTA! Y HA ECHADO
A ANDAR Y SU MARCHA
DE GIGANTES YA NO
SE DETENDRA HASTA
CONQUISTAR LA VER
DADERA INDEPENDEN
CIA

II DECLARACION
DE LA HABANA

*STATE-DIRECTED TASKS engage
many of Cuba's people, while others
seek a freer way of life in exile*

ARMED MILITIAWOMAN does guard duty in Havana. In 1966 Castro had a militia of some 200,000, plus a regular army of 90,000, well-equipped with Communist-bloc weapons.

DEPARTING REFUGEES are assisted by Cuban soldiers as they embark for the U.S. After September 1965, Castro allowed most of those who wanted to leave the island to depart freely.

VOLUNTEER CANECUTTER hacks away with a machete during the sugar harvest. Initially the Castro regime neglected this vital crop, but a national effort later increased output.

ARISTOCRATIC LADIES gossip on the corner of a tree-lined Havana street. Most young people of this class have fled Cuba, but some older ones have preferred to stay in their homes.

DEDICATED STUDENTS preparing to teach primary grades receive their training in an open-air classroom. The novice teachers will be assigned to schools in rural mountain areas.

Students hover over their teacher as he illustrates a principle of harmony during a class at San Juan's new Conservatory of Music.

The conservatory is headed by the renowned cellist Pablo Casals.

9

Experiment in Reform

A NEW feeling of hope is spreading among the people of the Caribbean islands; its source is their belief that opportunity, so long absent from their lives, exists at last. The feeling is still tentative in most of the West Indies, but in Puerto Rico it is surging; for in Puerto Rico the news has penetrated to the deepest mountain retreat that there is work to be found, either in new factories on the island or, after a cheap and swift flight, in the United States.

Only a few years ago Puerto Rico was a teeming, starving tropical slum. During 400 years of Spanish rule, the Puerto Ricans had learned to live as second-class citizens. Nothing the bumbling American benevolence had done since 1898 had improved their status; they had merely become hungrier and more numerous. Whereas the people of the other island colonies might think of themselves variously as English, French or Dutch citizens, few Puerto Ricans felt such direct identification with either Spain or the United States. By the 1930s their relations with the United States had deteriorated to the point where extremists were shooting and the U.S. Congress was considering jettisoning the colony. Most Puerto Rican intellectuals were clamoring for independence, even though the experiences of the island republics to the west offered little encouragement for believing that such a course would benefit Puerto Ricans.

THEN, in 1940, in a surprising election, the people of Puerto Rico voted for a detailed and specific legislative program proffered by a new political party. It was a bold proposal calling for the implementation of a stringent, but never before enforced, U.S. law limiting the size of the great sugar estates. The program was supported by President Franklin D. Roosevelt, and as its provisions one by one became law, and as the island's economy strengthened during World War II, conditions began to improve. In 1950, seeing a chance to divest itself of some of the responsibility and stigma of colonialism, Congress passed Public Law 600, granting Puerto Ricans the right to write their own constitution and pass their own laws.

Since that time Puerto Rico has developed a unique relationship with the United States that lies somewhere between protectorate and statehood. It is called "commonwealth status." It gives Puerto Ricans freedom to run their own affairs within the limits of the United States Constitution while providing the U.S. with a military base and a duty-free market for mainland products. As a commonwealth, Puerto Rico has cast aside its despair, reduced its birth rate and vastly increased the personal income of its citizens. Its loudest political agitators are calling not for independence but for an even closer relationship with the United States: they believe the island should become the 51st state of the Union. Puerto Rico calls itself, accurately, a "showcase for democracy"; its flourishing program of industrialization, "Operation Bootstrap," is studied by planners from infant nations around the world, and Washington finds the island a useful example when urging reform on reluctant Latin American nations.

Under Public Law 600, which was originally drafted in Puerto Rico and later ratified by the Puerto Rican voters, the islanders are U.S. citizens with all the rights of citizenship except two: the right to vote in national elections while residing on the island and the right to have a voting representative in Congress. They also have all the obligations of citizenship (including military service) except payment of federal income taxes. The federal government bestows benefits as if Puerto Rico were a state, disbursing grants-in-aid for hospitals, housing, roads and airports. Since the island is inside the U.S. customs barrier, Puerto Rican products reach mainland markets duty-free; and when federal excise taxes are imposed, the receipts are refunded to the commonwealth treasury—for rum alone these averaged close to $6 million a month by 1966.

THE people of Puerto Rico had previously demonstrated little genius for workable reform. From the early days, Puerto Rican society had been stratified, with a scattering of the rich—some of whom became millionaires in the sugar boom following World War I—divided from the poor by a small class of professional men. There had been a few gestures toward reform: a group had advocated self-government as early as 1823; but as late as 1868 *el grito de Lares* (the cry of Lares), a declaration of independence by a band of patriots in a small hill town, was all but forgotten after a few days. As the century waned, Puerto Rico spawned its pantheon of heroes: Eugenio María de Hostos, José de Diego, Román Baldorioty de Castro, Román Emeterio Betances, Manuel Fernández Juncos and the eminent Luis Muñoz Rivera, whose son became the island's first elected governor. They were poets, orators and dreamers who fulminated against the inequities of Spanish colonialism and formed party after party devoted to the cause of autonomy.

By mischance their activities became confused with those of an anti-Spanish secret society, *la boicotizadora*, which destroyed much

Spanish-owned property; and during the "terrible year" of 1887, both groups suffered *los compontes*—repressive measures ranging from censorship of the press to midnight arrests and torture. A decade later, in a wave of liberalism that followed one of Madrid's changing political tides, Puerto Rico was granted autonomy. Whether the new status would have survived another shift of government in Spain will never be known, for the island came into U.S. hands the next year, after the Spanish-American War.

THE social patterns of the Spanish colony are still reflected today, however wanly. The Spanish planter thought of himself as a hidalgo, or nobleman, and of the Puerto Rican people as peons. He expected the peons to show him slavish devotion. When he had money, he spent it on pleasure, for there was nothing more durable to be bought; his parties, complete with imported orchestras, could last for weeks. The hidalgo ruled his domain by gun and whip, but he left his children to be spoiled by his wife—he had a manly disrespect for women but a boyish reverence for motherhood. The island was a place to be barely tolerated, and he never became entirely assimilated.

From the beginning the hidalgos suffered as only poor relations can suffer. When they mined out the island's meager veins of gold, early in the 16th Century, the Crown sternly forbade them to leave the island. As planters they fared almost as badly; crops that managed to survive hurricanes and insect blights might rot in warehouses because years sometimes passed between visits by Spanish merchantmen. Since Spanish policy forbade trading with other nations, smuggling became a respectable way of life, and the hidalgo's propensity to lawlessness fattened into a streak of anarchism that has never disappeared.

In a strange convergence of attitudes, both the wealthy hidalgos and the penniless peons who swarmed about their estates became convinced that their unhappiness was somehow imposed by their immediate superiors. The hidalgos blamed the administrators in Madrid;

the peons blamed the hidalgos. Neither class seriously considered revolution, because neither had sufficient experience to know what it was missing. The planters, moreover, cherished the belief that they were still members of the society that was the cause of their resentment. The peons' resentments had been softened into submissiveness by centuries of degradation; the only changes they could remember had been for the worse.

Concerted action was next to impossible for a people to whom planning beyond tomorrow seemed pointless. Most of their violence took place when they were in rum; then, perhaps at a country dance, an imagined or real insult would be followed by a sudden ominous silence and the exit of the offended man and his friends—the men usually left their machetes under the entrance stairs—and their return to do battle. It was these generally peaceable peasants of the Puerto Rican hills, however, who became the spine of the only revolution that Puerto Rico ever had, that election day in 1940 when they dared tell the plantation owners that they intended to run their own affairs.

THESE peasants are called *jíbaros*. They are the lean and leathery descendants of Spaniards who took to the hills, many of them to evade military service or the law. Because so many of them were chary of authority, they scattered as widely as they could through the steep hills, learning from the Indians how to live off the land with a minimum of effort—and a resultant minimum of comfort. Their isolation was effective. Uninfluenced by the waves of new settlers from abroad, the most isolated *jíbaros* speak in an idiom which resembles the Castilian of some four centuries ago (their urban brothers speak a Spanish increasingly influenced by American slang). The *jíbaros* are famous for their suspiciousness and shrewdness as well as for their generosity and hospitality. To outwit a *jíbaro*, the saying goes, get another *jíbaro;* to outwit two *jíbaros*, you need the devil.

When, early in the 19th Century, the plantation owners began to seek workers from the hills, many of the *jíbaro* families became semi-migratory. The workers took their wives and children to company houses on the coast for *zafra*, the sugar harvest, then to the eastern mountains for the tobacco harvest or to the western mountains for the coffee harvest. Some of the planters allowed peons to take home all the vegetable produce they could carry at the day's end and in addition paid them 25 cents apiece. It added up to more than they could glean from working their own little farms, and they could buy clothes on credit from the company store and sometimes a chunk of salt pork to put in their rice and beans. If the crop was poor, the planter would lay them off and they would wind up in debt to the store, the interest accumulating until the next season, and so on, in a deepening spiral.

IT is easy to see why the palm-thatched house —the *bohio*—of one of these traveling laborers looked impermanent and unlovely on its crooked stilts above the muddy earth. It was not much in the first place—a pair of rooms for the whole family (which usually increased at the rate of a baby a year) and a smoke-blackened cookroom behind. A man's possessions—a woven-vine hammock and a calabash bowl, and perhaps a fighting cock—went with him. The earth took care, more or less, of his sanitary requirements. The peasants went barefoot; most of them had hookworm and the resultant crippling anemia. Most of them also suffered from ill-diagnosed but deadly fevers, pox, headaches and "stomach trouble." In the absence of doctors, the *jíbaros* bought patent medicines or summoned untrained *curanderos* or, if they believed in spiritualism, "healing mediums."

Just before the outbreak of World War II, Puerto Rican society had sunk to depths from which it seemed unlikely to climb. The despair of the period was reflected in the activities of the fanatical *Nacionalista* party, once a political force but subsequently reduced to fringe status by its failure at the polls in 1932. Led by the brilliant but implacable terrorist Pedro Albizu Campos, the *Nacionalistas* waged guerrilla warfare against the government (which they described as "illegal"). Their activities led to the Ponce Massacre on Palm Sunday, 1937. It is uncertain to this day who fired the first shot, but nervous policemen opened fire on *Nacionalista* demonstrators, and that Palm Sunday ended with about 200 civilians—and a few police—dead and wounded. (In 1950 the *Nacionalistas* staged an abortive revolution which included armed attacks on the governor's residence in San Juan and on Blair House in Washington, then the temporary residence of President Harry S. Truman. In 1954 four *Nacionalistas* fired wildly onto the floor of the House of Representatives. Albizu died in a guarded hospital room in 1965 and his burial was attended by Puerto Ricans of all political shades.

The Depression of the 1930s had reduced whole families to starvation. The files of relief agencies yield heartbreaking stories of that period: for example, that of a man who regularly begged a bucket of slops from a garbage truck, saying it was for his pig. Investigators found that his family was eating the garbage. The great exodus to the mainland had not yet begun. (In peak years it would number more than 75,000 islanders, giving New York a greater Puerto Rican population—600,000—than any Puerto Rican city.) The economy was in the grip of big American corporations which had bought up the sugar industry. Four corporations alone controlled 166,000 acres, despite a provision of the Foraker Act of 1900 that prohibited a corporation from controlling more than 500 acres.

MANY planters sold their land to the corporations and ran through their receipts; the planters who had held onto their land grew cane and lived on whatever the corporations felt like paying them for it. The peons earned starvation wages half the year and nothing at all for the other half. The legislature was firmly controlled by the corporations; those voters who were not intimidated by employers—the 150,000 unemployed—were paid from 50 cents to two dollars apiece to vote right. The Puerto Rico Reconstruction Administration had become demoralized, and the United States-appointed governor, General Blanton Winship, apparently could think of nothing more constructive than to turn the island into a quaint paradise for tourists.

Chief hope for reform was the young ex-senator Luis Muñoz Marín, who was Puerto Rico's first elected governor from 1948 until his retirement in 1964. He founded a new political party with a daring platform based on social and economic improvement at home. The program included not only enforcing the 500-acre law but bringing the sugar industry under public utility laws, distributing appropriated land to homeless peasants, and various other measures. To secure these promises, the party's candidates were required to swear in public to vote for them. Muñoz' organization was named the Popular Democratic party and was given a slogan, "Bread, Land and Liberty," and a symbol, the countryman's loose straw hat, the *pava*.

LIKE his father a poet and a journalist, Muñoz Marín had a thorough understanding of the peasant practicality and love of wit, and he had the quickness of mind to make use of his understanding. His election campaigns in the interior of Puerto Rico, rich in colorful examples, have been described by the island's unofficial English-language historian, Earl Parker Hanson, in his books *Transformation* and *Puerto Rico: Land of Wonders*. During the first campaign, for instance, one *jíbaro* claimed that Muñoz must be a man of the people because he drank Coca-Cola from a bottle. "Not so fast," said Muñoz. In the first place, there had been no glass handy and he was thirsty; in the second, if drinking out of bottles was enough to win an election, all the politicians would be doing it; and in the third, the people should vote for principles, not personalities. He himself would explain the principles. He pointed out how powerful the vote was in obtaining real benefits for the people—and in turning the politicos out of office if they did not deliver

what they had promised—and argued that this was worth more than the old two-dollar voting bribe, although he admitted that that kind of money was hard enough to come by. "You can't have the two dollars *and* justice," he told them.

In town after town the *jíbaro* population learned the principles of democratic elections from Muñoz' own lips, from phonograph recordings of his voice, from his articles in his rural newspaper, *El Batey* (The Dooryard). The *jíbaros* discovered that the message touched their pride as Muñoz' personality touched their hearts, and in 1940 they voted the Popular Democrats into a majority in the legislature.

This could have accomplished nothing if Roosevelt had appointed a typical colonial governor. The new man, Rexford Guy Tugwell, was, however, sympathetic to the movement, and this made him unpopular among many groups in Washington. Tugwell's critics, remembering that he had been one of Roosevelt's brain trust, thought him a dangerous radical. The conservative press in Puerto Rico launched attacks which lasted through Tugwell's five years in office, and cries of "socialism" rose on all sides. But Muñoz said, "We are neither radical nor conservative; we are realists," and the reform program gradually became law. The sophisticated political scientist and ex-brain truster had little in common with the inspired Latin American dreamer, but their ideals were almost identical, and there can be little doubt that some of Muñoz' mastery of administration was learned from Tugwell.

WORLD WAR II dramatically underlined Puerto Rico's need for economic diversification. Nazi submarine warfare was tragically effective during the early months of the war in the Caribbean. Puerto Rico, like the other islands, was faced with the possibility of starving to death if it could not import food. The enemy raiders capitalized on the United States' failure to win over its Latin neighbors, using the thinly populated islands off the Central American coast as refueling depots. As supply ship after supply ship was sunk en route to Puerto Rico, the shortage of food was matched by increasing unemployment; the building trades ran out of materials, and the island's second-largest industry, needlework, collapsed because its products could not be shipped to market.

When more ships began to get through safely, Puerto Rico's rum industry began to thrive —mainland distillers had converted to munitions work and the demand for liquor was heavy—and the Puerto Rican treasury profited handsomely. The Tugwell-Muñoz government accelerated decolonialization by completing the takeover of water, power and public transportation companies. The government's chief interest, however, lay in the liberation of sugar land, and it now became possible to make good on that campaign promise. A court action that had been started in 1936 had finally resulted in a ruling favorable to the government, which thereupon went about the business of divesting the sugar corporations of illegally controlled acreage. Bearing in mind the tragic errors in Haiti, where the land had been divided into plots too small to support their owners, the government purchased the condemned land outright and operated some of the farms on a profit-sharing basis, selling others to small farmers on long-term loans. The sugar corporations continued to own and operate their mills, using their own cane plus that delivered by surrounding planters.

THE effects of this program remain to be finally evaluated, but it is clear that sugar is losing ground as Puerto Rico's most important product. The planners turn deaf ears to cries that they are ruining the economy. The desired side effect—diversification into food crops—is slowly getting under way.

Even if Puerto Rico were to devote all of its soil to food crops, however, the island still would not be able to support its teeming population. For years, industrialization had been recommended as the only solution, but nobody had figured out how to get a successful program started: moneyed Puerto Ricans invariably invested elsewhere, and foreign capital could be raised only to grow sugar cane. The answer was found in the formation of the Economic Development Administration, called Fomento, backed by a Government Development Bank. Fomento salesmen invaded the U.S. mainland to induce industries to establish subsidiaries on the island. As incentives they offered long-term exemptions on corporate income taxes, ready-made factories for sale or rent and payment of salaries for experts imported from the mainland to train local workers.

By 1966 there were more than 1200 factories in operation, and 75,000 new jobs had been created. Major industries were attracting secondary ones to supply manufacturing and merchandising needs—carton factories to provide packaging for the rum industry, for instance.

The social changes have been startling. Today a single factory in a small town may pay its employees more than the town's entire labor force previously earned. The added purchasing power is reflected in increased prosperity among merchants. Hoarded money starts to flow, civic pride is discovered, and there is an almost tangible surge of optimism.

AS the island economy improved, the government began to encourage tourism. The first step was construction of the $7.2 million Caribe Hilton in 1949, which has become one of the world's most profitable hotels. It has become the model for all American overseas hotels, but few of them have equaled the quality of its design—a product of Puerto Rican architects. It is still owned by Fomento and is operated by Hilton for a third of the profits. Puerto Rico now has 33 resort hotels in operation, but the tourists, nudged by recurring cold weather in Florida, the cold shoulder in Cuba, and bargain-rate flights, could use twice as many. San Juan, which at the end of World War II had no higher a skyline than it had had 400 years before, is now spiky with tall buildings, while in the depths of the Old City a restoration program is bringing back the beauty of mahogany balconies and masonry arches.

Looking back across the astonishingly few years, it would appear that Puerto Ricans were readier than anybody imagined to leap into the modern world. The Planning Board, which is responsible for predicting the future by extrapolating from the past, has sometimes been unable to keep its projections in focus: in 1959 more than a million passengers passed through San Juan's International Airport, the number predicted for 1965; the pell-mell growth of middle-class housing developments, which corrugate the landscape around every city, has overloaded the old roads that serve them; the sudden appearance of thousands of secondhand cars, combined with the Puerto Rican's undiminished resistance to authority, has clogged even the modern traffic highways.

WITH the airlines' conversion to frequent and inexpensive jet flights, San Juan has come within practical commuting range of New York. A number of mainland citizens whose professions permit flexible schedules have left the United States to set up housekeeping in the semitropical exurbia while continuing to do business in the United States. Most of the blessings and curses of American middle-class life are now easily available. Mothers can enjoy such luxuries as diaper service, reducing salons and floor-a-second elevators to penthouse bars. Teen-age daughters can roll their hair in drum curlers from Woolworth's and head for a drive-in, confident they will find a film about go-go dancing or monsters from outer space, while the boys tear up the pavement in souped-up V-8s. It is also possible to tune in on one of the nine television or 35 radio stations. One anachronism is the unreliable telephone service, in which only the billing department is really efficient. The growing middle class is adapting rapidly to these aspects of the revolution, although here and there a voice is raised in an effort to salvage Puerto Rican culture before it is swallowed up, and there are occasional cries of "Yankee go home."

As the news of modern pleasures penetrates inland and the demands of industrialization

THE VIRGIN ISLANDS: TINY U.S. OUTPOST

The Virgin Islands were discovered by Columbus during his second voyage in 1493. Their name comes from the legend of St. Ursula, who is said to have made a pilgrimage to Rome accompanied by 10,999 virgins and to have been martyred, with all her companions, by Attila the Hun. To Columbus' crew it appeared that they were sailing among thousands of islands, and someone, perhaps Columbus himself, remembered the legend and named them the Virgins. There are, in fact, only about 100 islands, islets, cays and rocks in the Virgin Island group, but the name has stuck.

HISTORY

The islands soon became pawns of the rival colonial powers. During the 17th Century alone they were held at various times by France, England, Spain, Holland and Denmark. England and Denmark ended up sharing control of them, and the British still own about 30 of the islands. The Danes in 1917 sold their 50-odd islands to the United States for $25 million. Their value for the U.S. was primarily strategic: the islands command the Anegada Passage into the Caribbean and help protect the Panama Canal.

GOVERNMENT

The principal U.S. Virgin Islands are St. Croix, St. Thomas and St. John. The capital is Charlotte Amalie on St. Thomas. The chief executive is a governor appointed by the President of the U.S., but the Virgin Islanders are U.S. citizens and elect their own 11-man legislature. They do not, however, have a representative in Congress. The islands are classed as an "unincorporated territory."

ECONOMY

Once dependent on sugar, the islands now rely on tourists for their main livelihood. They do produce a considerable quantity of rum, however (1.4 million proof gallons in 1965), and also raise cattle and vegetables.

increase, the peasant population is gradually moving toward the cities. But the transplanted *jíbaro's* beloved hill country begins just a few minutes out of town, and he never misses a chance to drive out to assuage his passion for it. It would be impossible to document the sources of his feeling, but it is safe to say it does not strike him through his ears. Puerto Rico's bird population, as if fearing to reveal itself to the people it once fed, sings at dawn and falls silent; when darkness falls, there are the calls of the dinning insects and toads— some of which are curiously birdlike. Others are as harsh and brittle as castanets or a police whistle. From the side of a conical hill, a man can hear the indescribably peaceful aural effect of sheer distance, an effect whose chief component, despite the presence of 730 people per square mile, is yawning silence punctuated by a bark or cry from miles away. But judging from the relentless tumult of urban Puerto Rico, the people can take silence or leave it alone.

Visually, however, rural Puerto Rico is capable of arousing in the *jíbaro* a euphoria that does not diminish over the years. It is accompanied by the unreasonable conviction that he actually owns—or could own—everything he sees. It strikes him at sunrise, when the perfumes of the night-flowering jasmine and frangipani linger on the air, when the rising breeze breaks up the black predawn rain clouds and the sun converts them to pink-white puffs and dapples the hillsides. It strikes him again when a swift shower chills him—while allowing him a dazzling, distant glimpse of blue; or when a rare overcast moves across the island, leaving at the horizon a strip of electrical color dividing pewter clouds from the sullen sea; or merely when there are clouds inhabiting the sky, comforting him by their very presence, as he is comforted by the presence of people.

HE is comforted also by the fertility of the red earth. He knows he could plant an orange, grapefruit or lime tree by simply eating a fruit and spitting the seeds on the ground. His mango and avocado trees may bear only in the summer months, but the banana and its unsweet relatives of the plantain family bear fruit without reference to the season, and hidden in the ground are potatolike edibles such as the *ñame*, the cassava and the malanga. The coconut comforts him with sweet water to drink, and its palm fronds can be plaited into walls. He is intimate with the properties of weeds and grasses and may gather even the leafless, fleshy parasite called *fideíllo* or the decorative, pancake-shaped leaf of the sea grape to brew into broths to medicate an ailing member of his family. The smitten *jíbaro* takes pleasure in the lurid *flamboyán* and poinsettia trees as well as in the commonplace excesses of hibiscus

and bougainvillaea. But it is his instinct to resist encroaching nature; when he thinks the trees and shrubs are getting too big or too close, he hacks them back with his machete.

When he sees the necessity, however, the realistic Puerto Rican is not afraid to depart his overpopulated island—as he once departed his *bohío* to work in the planters' fields—but when he does he grieves for it. (One man's grief bubbled over to become a popular song called "Lamento Borincano." It expressed the yearning of the *jíbaro* so eloquently that it has practically become the commonwealth's second anthem.)

TODAY, however, Puerto Rico's image is changing in the eyes of its departed sons. In 1961, for the first time in a generation, the flow of people to the mainland reversed, and some 1,700 more Puerto Ricans returned to their island than left it. Despite the fact that a mainland recession was clearly a major factor in their return, the figures indicated that many of the exiles saw hope for themselves at home. This state of mind gratified the planners, but the economic implications dismayed them, for the people who leave Puerto Rico are mostly workers. If they should choose to stay home, the increase in the Puerto Rican labor pool could be disastrous. "Operation Bootstrap" has slowed the birth rate, partly because of the indisputable fact that people with jobs have fewer children. In addition, large numbers of Puerto Rican women, contrary to all expectations, have voluntarily sought to limit the number of their children by contraceptive means and—where medically prescribed—by sterilization.

But though the birth rate has been slowed, so has the death rate, and the population continues to increase. Fortunately, in 1966 the net flow appeared to have turned northward again. For all the U.S. economic and technological aid, it would appear that the United States' most important contribution to Puerto Rican prosperity is its absorption of Puerto Ricans. Without this, the achievements of the island planners might simply be overwhelmed.

The giant petrochemical plant of the Commonwealth Oil Refining Company in Puerto Rico is the world's largest installation of its kind.

The Near-Miracle of Puerto Rico's New Wealth

In the last two decades Puerto Rico has made an amazing economic about-face. Once desperately poor, it has become one of the West Indies' most prosperous islands. With government assistance, more than 1,200 new factories have been opened since 1947. Per capita income rose from $121 a year in 1940 to $830 in 1966. With prosperity have come not just material benefits but a new interest in education, a new energy in the arts and a buoyant faith in the future.

CHEERFUL ROOM with bright curtains and flooring surrounds José Ortíz, a Division of Community Education "group organizer" *(above)*, and his sons as they watch television.

BLACKBOARD LECTURE is given a small group of villagers by Ortíz. Like other group organizers, he travels from town to town teaching new methods of meeting community problems.

RURAL HOME nears completion as neighbors pitch in to construct a terrace *(above)*. Under Puerto Rico's self-help housing plan, the government supplies expert advice and loans for materials while the homeowner and his neighbors do the construction. Usually made of reinforced concrete, more than 10,000 rural homes have been raised under this plan since 1950.

A FRESH LOOK spreads as the economic boom manifests itself in new homes, offices, hotels and manufacturing plants

RESTORED HOUSES, some excellent examples of Spanish colonial architecture, line a street in Old San Juan. The government gives tax concessions to owners who do restoring.

CROWDED SKYLINE of modern office buildings and hotels overshadows San Juan's homes and churches *(right)*. Investment in new construction has almost trebled in the last decade.

HOUSING DEVELOPMENT, where children ride horseback, provides homes for Puerto Rico's growing middle class. New houses are being built on the island at the rate of 46 per day.

INDUSTRIAL PLANT built by the Puerto Rican subsidiary of Parke, Davis & Co. includes a glass-walled employees' cafeteria *(below)*. Many big U.S. firms have plants on the island.

BLIGHTED AREAS still exist, dimming somewhat the luster of recent achievements, although the island government is pressing an energetic clearance program designed to eradicate the slums

SEA-WASHED SLUM ironically called La Perla, or The Pearl, is only a five-minute walk from San Juan's Capitol. Many of La Perla's tottering shacks are built of packing crates, drift-wood and old advertising signs. Situated next to the water, they are sometimes shattered by storms but they grow up again.

WEATHERED SHANTIES of a crowded slum called El Fan-guito (The Little Mud Hole) cluster behind one of San Juan's busy shopping streets, Avenida Ponce de León, with its big First Federal Building *(right, background)*. Slum dwellers are gradually being transferred to new low-cost housing projects.

142

10

Reaching for Maturity

A SILHOUETTE of events in the life of the Caribbean islands would form a series of infrequent peaks separated by broad valleys. The peaks would correspond to those periods when foreign powers, for one reason or another, focused their attention on the area. For example, after the initial disappointment over the amount of gold to be found there, the islands became important in the 16th Century as harbors of refuge and supply for Spanish treasure ships; then they became a source of wealth and power for those who could get possession of sugar land. For a time they were strategically important as parts of the defensive perimeter around the Panama Canal; during World War II they simply became places to be denied to the Nazis. In the 1960s the area again became important as a focal point of U.S.-Soviet rivalry. The valleys, on the other hand, would represent the long periods when nothing historically more interesting than the growth of money crops took place.

As the European proprietors lost interest in the Caribbean, the United States might have been expected to move forcefully into the area. But that nation took control only of Puerto Rico and a few of the Virgin Islands and exerted its influence on other islands by different means. Yet the U.S. impact was eventually broad, although the imperial pattern did not repeat itself. It was the stimulus provided by American troops in the area in World War II, and the population movements occasioned by the war, that led the islanders, already becoming aware of themselves as individuals, to an awareness of their potential political importance.

FURTHER encounters with international politics, like those which were seen in Cuba in 1962, must be expected from time to time in the future. Communism's prospects in the Caribbean are nevertheless shaky. Martinique and Guadeloupe contain many people who have been affected by Communist ideals and who vote for Communist candidates. But like the leaders of their mother country, the leaders of the two islands are too independent-minded to be taken over easily by an outside power. Haiti, conveniently located next to Cuba, could fall in any direction but would present overwhelming organizational and financial problems to any new regime. The outspoken resentment of Western racialism expressed by Trinidad's premier, Eric Williams, has led some observers to worry lest that new nation move toward the Soviet camp, but Trinidad would have more to lose than to gain by such a step; Trinidad's destiny, brightened by a reasonable hope for economic stability based on its oil resources, appears to be more that of a local leader than of a foreign country's satellite.

Williams is clearly aware of Trinidad's potential role. He has spoken in favor of a confederation of British islands under Trinidad's leadership, and he has left the door open for the beginnings of such a community by inviting other islands to join the "unitary state" of Trinidad and Tobago; Grenada immediately applied for admission—thus illustrating the rapidity with which alignments in the area are shifting. As recently as 1962, the possibility of any form of unity between islands of different economic levels was so unacceptable that the Federation of the West Indies, loose as it was, foundered partly over that issue. The

rate of change, moreover, is rapidly accelerating.

Today, hopelessness is being replaced by discontent. In the islands, such a change is a positive one. Outbursts of unfocused rage have in recent years given way to strikes and other organized manifestations undertaken to achieve specific gains. On the personal level, the servility-sullenness pattern is being replaced by curiosity or aloofness; the American who has been accustomed in the past to get smiles just because he was friendly has begun to get speculative stares instead.

Other symptoms of the change are everywhere apparent. The individual has discovered that he wants some of the European's advantages—like clean clothes and a house of his own. The West Indian has found that the way to obtain these advantages is through higher wages, and that the way to higher wages is through the organizing of labor unions and political parties. Increasing success at this kind of cooperation has nourished a greater political awareness. The individual has at last discovered that by pooling his efforts with others he can exert noticeable pressure to affect the laws he lives by, and he is even beginning to think he can induce the outside world to pay attention to him.

IN addition, the West Indian who used to suffer secret shame because his ancestors were slaves is beginning to take pride in himself, in his racial background and in the emergence of the new nations of Africa. Africa has been transformed in his mind's eye from a word not to be mentioned to a place to be sought by some as a promised land and by others as a mine of half-forgotten customs that might add richness to life in the islands. While there are still people of colored skin who continue to shy away from the word "Negro" as something vaguely derogatory, the new intellectuals are discovering that self-esteem is embodied in a made-up word—*négritude*.

Another index of the change may be found in education. While school children once studied only European history, they have recently been learning in many areas about their own islands. Residents more frequently think of themselves now as "Grenadian," "St. Lucian," "Puerto Rican," "Aruban" and so forth, where formerly they thought of themselves as English, Spanish or Dutch. Even more significantly, they are beginning to think of themselves simply as "West Indians." The study of local history on the primary level has been paralleled by a growing interest in scholarly research that not only has begun to catalogue for the first time many patterns of behavior but also has given West Indians the dignity that comes from an understanding of themselves. From individual pride to general pride is a natural step, and today the leading trend of political thought is away from overseas entanglements; the West Indian is beginning to think of the area as an entity.

T HE process of self-examination has produced some fine literary works. Notable among these are the sardonic and vividly observed novels of life among island Negroes by George Lamming; the well-shaped creations of John Hearne; the poetry of Derek Walcott; and the professional work done by such young writers as Orlando Patterson, whose *Children of Sisyphus* won recognition at the First World Festival of Negro Arts in Dakar. Also demanding mention are the bitingly phrased histories and polemics by Eric Williams, and the fiery poetry of Martinique's Aimé Césaire.

Of all West Indian authors, perhaps the most significant is V. S. Naipaul, who in *The Middle Passage* looked with a fresh eye at British, Dutch and French islanders. "Trinidad considers itself, and is acknowledged by the other West Indian territories to be modern," he wrote. "To be modern is to ignore local products and to use those advertised in American magazines. . . . Modernity in Trinidad, then, turns out to be the extreme susceptibility of people who are unsure of themselves and . . . are eager for instruction. . . . Trinidad was and remains a materialist immigrant society, continually growing and changing, never settling into any pattern. . . . All this has combined to give it its special character, its ebullience and irresponsibility. And more: a tolerance which is more than tolerance: an indifference to virtue as well as to vice."

The West Indian Negroes are nowhere analyzing themselves more bitterly than in Jamaica. The following is excerpted from a letter by a university student to Kingston's *Sunday Gleaner:* "The Negro as a rule shows preference for people of other races. . . . There are comparatively few Negro parents who object when their children take partners of another race. . . . If anybody thinks the black man is satisfied with the status quo, he is mistaken. . . . He wants respect and recognition for his status. . . . He wants money and economic stability as a race. . . . If a change cannot be effected by social evolution then it will become necessary to use the methods the white man has used so successfully in so many countries. Either way we are going to get what we want."

A more considered attitude is shown in recent publications of the area-wide New World group; they advocate change—but change without ideological affiliations.

The new-found introspection of West Indian intellectuals has brought some of them to regard the 1962 breakup of the Federation of the West Indies as only an interruption of the development of closer cooperation between all of the Caribbean territories. Advocates of a Caribbean federation have come to feel that whatever the sacrifice of individual island autonomy, the West Indies desperately needs some sort of common political and economic unit to deal effectively with the islands' multiplicity of problems. Forces for unification are weak at present—the war-born Caribbean Organization folded in 1964—but future economic pressures might revitalize the drive for unity.

U NFORTUNATELY, the objections to unification are formidable. If, for instance, the essential customs union were to be established without destroying present allegiances, it would be necessary to erect some other tariff device to keep dutiable products from flowing freely into the mother countries. Even the free movement of people from island to island raises problems. Historically, this has been a touchy point. In addition, it would be hard to convince certain islanders to give up such very real benefits as the French social security—to say nothing of their prized French citizenship —in return for some vague future rewards.

ALMOST every island is suspicious of for- eigners, even those from next door. This is particularly true of islands where there are good jobs, as there are in Trinidad's oil re- fineries. Barriers to immigration exist on every island. The result of the restrictions, like that of the monopolistic trade policies of colonial days, is smuggling—except that today's smug- gled items are people. There is a steady, illegal stream of movement from the British Virgin Islands to the U.S. Virgin Islands, from Grena- da to Trinidad, from Antigua to St. Thomas.

The creation of a truly united West Indies— a United States of the Caribbean—is of course only a distant dream. Optimists still think it could be achieved—perhaps in a genera- tion. It would take that long because it would be necessary to resolve such basic conflicts as government by democracy—in which the local public approves whatever steps are tak- en—with an economy dependent on foreign markets and suppliers—in which the decisions are made elsewhere on the basis of strange and perhaps secret criteria. The optimists neverthe- less believe it can be done. First steps would be either toward independence within the pro- tection of the ex-mother country, or toward the "free association" relationship exemplified by Puerto Rico.

All proposals for joint economic effort are naturally for the distant future. At present, for- midable problems remain. In the late 1960s, the Caribbean territories could be thought of as divided, like the peoples that have so long in- habited them, into several economic strata. On one level was Puerto Rico, actively governing itself within the protective embrace of the

United States and apparently on the road to a better life, and even prosperity, for its people. Others on this level included the islands that had achieved independence and could, with ex- isting natural resources and friendly markets for their produce and manufactures, hope for sta- ble societies within the foreseeable future: Ja- maica, Trinidad and Tobago, and possibly the Dominican Republic. A center of international controversy but basically sound economically was Cuba.

Far less comfortable was almost the entire crescent of smaller British and French islands in the eastern Caribbean. There have been many suggestions that the British islands find a protector in Canada, possibly through a relationship resembling that between Puerto Rico and the United States, but Canada has never been particularly receptive to the idea. Martinique and Guadeloupe were assured of a market and of price subsidies for their crops by their association with France, but unem- ployment was great and caused periodic unrest in both islands. At the bottom of the list was independent Haiti, with no strong overseas ties and with no outward indication of realizing that drastic measures would be required to in- sure mere survival.

THE array of possibilities was bewildering, and no observer could say which of them —if any—might eventually become reality. It seemed clear, however, that the West Indies were at last oriented more toward the future than the past; even the poor and unlettered country dwellers had come a long way from slavery. It might be said that the islands of the West Indies had lived through their seemingly endless, careless childhood, during which they were scorned or ignored by their own par- ents. In the late 1960s they were beginning to face responsibilities, admittedly in some con- fusion and unpredictability, as befitted matur- ing youths. If they reach the adulthood that they should, they might well become the para- dise that Christopher Columbus declared them to be, so many years ago.

Dominicans watch television at their local store. Next page: Schooner prows shade the waterfront market in Willemstad, Curaçao.

AN EAGER QUEST for knowledge and for social and economic betterment . . .

. . . underscores the West Indian's demand to be respected as a human being with

his own indigenous customs and his own right to a larger share in the modern world

Appendix

HISTORICAL DATES

B.C.

1000 or before Various Indian peoples—among them the Caribs, Arawaks and Ciboney—spread throughout the Caribbean

A.D.

1492 Columbus makes his historic landfall at San Salvador. On this first voyage, he also discovers Hispaniola and Cuba

1493 Pope Alexander VI issues papal bulls dividing the New World between Spain and Portugal; the entire Caribbean is assigned to Spain

1493-1504 Columbus makes three further voyages, discovering virtually all the remaining major islands

1506 First sugar mill in the Caribbean is established on Hispaniola. French ships raid Spanish vessels and colonies, and undeclared war breaks out between France and Spain, first of a series of formal and informal conflicts between the European colonial powers that are to plague the area for more than two centuries

1510 The Spanish Crown grants authorization for the importation of slaves to the area

1562 The Portuguese monopoly of the African slave trade is broken when John Hawkins, an English privateer, buys three cargoes of slaves in West Africa and sells them in the Caribbean

1586 Sir Francis Drake of England raids Santo Domingo and sacks Cartagena

1588 Defeat of the Spanish Armada off Britain by an English fleet led by Drake and Hawkins has far-reaching effects on the Caribbean; Spain's hegemony is henceforth on the wane

1623 The British settle St. Christopher (St. Kitts), their first West Indies colony

1634-1640 The Dutch seize Aruba, Bonaire and Curaçao from the Spanish, also settle Saba, Sint Eustatius and Sint Maarten

1635 The French begin settlement of Martinique and Guadeloupe

c.1645 Intensive cultivation of sugar cane begins in the British and French colonies. In consequence, the importation of slaves is stepped up. French slavers enter the trade and are shortly joined by an increasing number of Englishmen

1685 Under pressure from investors fearful of slave revolts, Louis XIV of France promulgates the Code Noire, a document which assigns some rights to slaves but prescribes severe penalties for rebellion and flight

1760 Slaves revolt in Jamaica; the rebellion is put down harshly

1762-1763 The English occupy Havana, and Cuba awakens to the possibility of trading with countries other than Spain

1798-1804 Under the leadership of Toussaint L'Ouverture, slaves revolt in the French colony of Saint-Domingue on Hispaniola. The Republic of Haiti is established

1807 England declares the slave trade illegal; the French follow suit in 1818, the Spanish in 1820

1814-1815 With the end of the Napoleonic Wars in Europe, the Caribbean fighting among the colonial powers comes to a close

1822 Haitians invade and occupy the Spanish portion of Hispaniola

1833 The British declare slavery abolished in the British islands

1844 The Spanish part of Hispaniola revolts and throws off Haitian rule. The Dominican Republic is proclaimed

1848 France declares slavery abolished

1868-1878 Cubans revolt and declare independence; Spanish forces put down the rebellion

1886 Slavery is abolished in Cuba

1895 Another revolt against Spanish rule breaks out in Cuba

1898 The United States defeats Spain in the Spanish-American War; Spain loses Puerto Rico, Guam and the Philippines to the U.S. Cuba becomes independent

1901 The U.S. Platt Amendment asserts the right to intervene in Cuba to restore order

1906-1909 Unstable political situation in Cuba brings U.S. intervention

1915 After threats by France and Germany to collect their debts from near-bankrupt Haiti by force, the U.S. sends troops to occupy the country

1916 First oil refinery in the Caribbean is established on Curaçao. Collapse of organized government in the Dominican Republic precipitates a U.S. occupation

1917 The U.S. purchases St. Thomas, St. John, St. Croix and smaller Virgin Islands from Denmark for $25 million

1924 U.S. forces withdraw from the Dominican Republic. Gerardo Machado becomes president of Cuba, later rules as dictator

1930 Rafael Trujillo becomes president of the Dominican Republic

1933 Machado is forced to flee Cuba

1934 The U.S. repeals the Platt Amendment. U.S. occupation troops withdraw from Haiti

1940 Fulgencio Batista becomes president of Cuba

1946 Guadeloupe and Martinique become *départements* of France

1952 Batista seizes power in Cuba for a second time

1956 After a disastrous landing on the south coast of Cuba, Fidel Castro and a few followers escape to the Sierra Maestra

1957 François Duvalier becomes president of Haiti

1958 The Federation of the West Indies, a grouping of British islands, is established

1959 Batista flees into exile; Fidel Castro marches into Havana and assumes power

1961 Trujillo is assassinated in the Dominican Republic. In Haiti, Duvalier stages an election and announces that he has been elected to a second four-year term which will begin in 1963. Cuban exiles launch an unsuccessful invasion of their island at the Bay of Pigs on the south coast

1962 The Federation of the West Indies founders as its independence is about to be proclaimed; Jamaica and the "unitary state" of Trinidad and Tobago become independent nations. After a Russian arms and missile build-up in Cuba, the U.S. establishes a quasi-blockade of the island

1963 Juan Bosch is inaugurated president of the Dominican Republic after a democratic election

1964 Bosch deposed; goes into exile. Muñoz Marín retires from governorship of Puerto Rico, and Roberto Sanchez Vilella is elected governor

1965 Civil war flares in the Dominican Republic between pro- and anti-Bosch factions. U.S. marines land in Santo Domingo and are later absorbed into an O.A.S. peace-keeping force

1966 Bosch returns to the Dominican Republic but loses to Joaquín Balaguer in a new election

FOR FURTHER READING

CHAPTER 1: A PARADISE IN FERMENT

Clark, Sydney, *All the Best in the Caribbean*. Dodd, Mead, 1960.

Fermor, Patrick Leigh, *The Traveller's Tree*. Harper & Brothers, 1950.

Fodor, Eugene, *Fodor's Guide to the Caribbean, Bahamas and Bermuda*. David McKay, 1966.

Luke, Sir Harry, *Caribbean Circuit*. Nicholson P. Watson, London, 1950.

Smith, Bradley, *Escape to the West Indies*. Alfred A. Knopf, 1961.

Tannehill, Ivan Ray, *Hurricanes, Their Nature and History*. Princeton University Press, 1956.

CHAPTER 2: THE RACE FOR RICHES

Arciniegas, German, *Caribbean: Sea of the New World*. Alfred A. Knopf, 1946.

Carrington, C. E., *The British Overrseas*. Cambridge University Press, 1950.

Crouse, Nellis M., *The French Struggle for the West Indies*. Columbia University Press, 1943.

Herring, Hubert, *A History of Latin America*. Alfred A. Knopf, 1961.

Morison, Samuel Eliot, *Admiral of the Ocean Sea*. Little, Brown & Co., 1942.

Parry, J. H., and P. M. Sherlock, *A Short History of the West Indies*. St. Martin's Press, 1960.

Roberts, W. Adolphe, *The French in the West Indies*. Bobbs-Merrill, 1942. *The Caribbean: The Story of Our Sea of Destiny*. Bobbs-Merrill, 1940.

CHAPTER 3: THE IMPACT OF SLAVERY

Davidson, Basil, *Black Mother*. Atlantic-Little, Brown, 1961.

Deerr, Noel, *The History of Sugar*. Chapman, London, 1950.

Herskovits, Melville T., *The Myth of the Negro Past*. Harper & Brothers, 1941.

Mannix, Daniel P., and Malcolm Cooley, *Black Cargoes*. Viking, 1962.

Tannenbaum, Frank, *Slave and Citizen*. Vintage Books, 1963.

CHAPTERS 4 AND 5: RELIGION AND THE ARTS

Deren, Maya, *The Divine Horsemen*. Thames, London, 1953.

Herskovits, Melville T., *Life in a Haitian Valley*. Alfred A. Knopf, 1937.

Herskovits, Melville T. and Frances S., *Trinidad Village*. Alfred A. Knopf, 1947.

Lamming, George, *Session of Adventure*. Collins, 1960.

Métraux, Alfred, *Voodoo*. Oxford University Press, 1959.

Thoby-Marcelin, Philippe, and Pierre Marcelin, *Beast of the Haitian Hills*. Rinehart, 1946.

CHAPTER 6: THE FRENCH ISLANDS

Leyburn, James G., *The Haitian People*. Yale University Press, 1955.

Rodman, Selden, *Haiti: The Black Republic*. Devin-Adair, 1961.

CHAPTER 7: THE BRITISH ISLANDS

Ayearst, Morley, *The British West Indies*. New York University Press, 1960.

Burns, Sir Alan, *History of the British West Indies*. George Allen and Unwin, London, 1954.

Connell, Neville, *A Short History of Barbados*. Barbados Museum and Historical Society, 1960.

Roberts, W. Adolphe, *Jamaica, the Portrait of an Island*. Coward-McCann, 1955.

Williams, Eric, *History of the People of Trinidad and Tobago*. PNM Publishing Co., Port of Spain, 1962.

CHAPTER 8: THE SPANISH ISLANDS

MacGaffey, Wyatt, and Clifford R. Barnett, *Cuba: Its People, Its Society, Its Culture*. Human Relations Area Files Press, New Haven, Conn., 1962.

Phillips, R. Hart, *Cuba: Island of Paradox*. McDowell, Obolensky, 1959.

Roberts, W. Adolphe, *Havana: The Portrait of a City*. Coward-McCann, 1953.

Welles, Sumner, *Naboth's Vineyard: The Dominican Republic, 1844-1924*. Payson and Clarke, Ltd., New York, 1928.

CHAPTER 9: PUERTO RICO

Brameld, Theodore A., *Remaking of a Culture: Life and Education in Puerto Rico*. Harper & Brothers, 1959.

Hanson, Earl Parker, *Puerto Rico, Land of Wonders*. Alfred A. Knopf, 1960.

Mathews, Thomas G., *Puerto Rican Politics and the New Deal*. University of Florida Press, 1960.

Mintz, Sidney W., *Worker in the Cane: A Puerto Rican Life History*. Yale University Press, 1960.

Rand, Christopher, *The Puerto Ricans*. Oxford University Press, New York, 1958.

CHAPTER 10: THE FUTURE

Clark, Gerald, *The Coming Explosion in Latin America*. David McKay, 1963.

Naipaul, V. S., *The Middle Passage: The Caribbean Revisited*. Andre Deutsch, Ltd., London, 1962.

Proudfoot, Mary, *Britain and the United States in the Caribbean*. Frederick A. Praeger, 1953.

CARIBBEAN RECORDINGS

In addition to the widely distributed recordings of such Caribbean music as Afro-Cuban, calypso and steel-band, there are recordings of less familiar music and speech that provide invaluable insights into island life. The author recommends those listed below. In the list, the word "Cook" designates Cook Laboratories, Inc., 101 Second Street, Stamford, Connecticut, the word "Folk" designates Folkways Records, 121 West 47th Street, New York, New York. All records are 33⅓ RPM LPs. The catalogue number follows the publisher's name.

GENERAL

Caribbean Folk Music, Vol. 1. Folk, FE 4533.

Caribbean Dances. Folk, FW 6840.

TRINIDAD

Jump Up Carnival. Cook, 1072.

Calypso Lore and Legend (spoken, no music). Cook, 5016.

Drums of Trinidad. Cook, 1045.

East Indian Drums of Tunapuna. Cook, 5018.

Bamboo-Tamboo, Bongo and Belair. Cook, 5017.

HAITI

Creole Songs of Haiti. Folk, FW 6833.

Haiti Confidential. Cook, 1022.

JAMAICA

Jamaican Folk Songs. Folk, FW 6846.

BRITISH WEST INDIES

Anancy Stories. Cook, E 105.

Songs of the British West Indies. Folk, FW 8809.

PUERTO RICO

Folk Songs and Dances from Puerto Rico. Folk, FW 8802.

CUBA

Musica de Cuba pre-Castro. Cook, 1083.

MARTINIQUE

Martinique. Cook, 1021.

MAJOR POLITICAL UNITS OF THE WEST INDIES

PLACE	POP.	AREA	OWNERSHIP HISTORY	POLITICAL STATUS
CUBA	7,200,000	44,164 sq. mi.	Settled by the Spanish, briefly occupied by the English, became independent 1898	Republic
DOMINICAN REPUBLIC	3,451,700	19,129 sq. mi.	Settled by the Spanish, conquered by Haiti 1822, won independence 1844	Republic
HAITI	4,660,000	10,714 sq. mi.	Spanish until 1697, when France obtained the western third of Hispaniola; won independence 1804	Republic
PUERTO RICO	2,622,700	3,423 sq. mi.	Colonized by the Spanish, ceded to the U.S. 1898	Self-governing commonwealth in association with the U.S.
U.S. VIRGINS (ST. THOMAS, ST. CROIX, ST. JOHN)	36,412	132 sq. mi.	Held at different times by Spain, the Netherlands, France, Britain and Denmark; purchased by the U.S. from Denmark in 1917	U.S. territory
JAMAICA	1,700,000	4,411 sq. mi.	Spanish until 1509, captured by the British 1655, granted independence 1962	Member British Commonwealth
TRINIDAD AND TOBAGO	854,342	1,980 sq. mi.	Trinidad: Spanish until ceded to Great Britain 1802. Tobago: first settled by the Dutch 1632; became a British possession 1814. Both granted independence 1962	Member British Commonwealth
ANTIGUA, BARBUDA, REDONDA	61,664	170 sq. mi.	Antigua: colonized by the British 1632. Barbuda and Redonda: colonized by the British 1661, now dependencies of Antigua	British colony
BAHAMAS	138,500	4,405 sq. mi.	Discovered 1492 by Christopher Columbus, settled by British in 1648 and ceded to Britain by Spain in 1783	British colony
BARBADOS	244,165	166 sq. mi.	Settled by British 1627	British colony
CAYMAN ISLANDS	8,588	100 sq. mi.	Grand Cayman settled by the British 1734; Little Cayman and Cayman Brac settled by the British 1833	British colony
DOMINICA	65,165	289 sq. mi.	Settled by the French, conquered by the British 1763, recaptured by the French 1778, restored to Britain 1783	British colony
GRENADA AND CARRIACOU	88,000	133 sq. mi.	Grenada: settled by the French 1650, held alternately by Britain and France, restored to Britain 1784. Carriacou and other southern Grenadines now dependencies of Grenada	British colony
MONTSERRAT	13,430	32 sq. mi.	First colonized by the Irish 1632, briefly held by the French, came under British control 1783	British colony
ST. CHRISTOPHER, NEVIS, ANGUILLA	60,451	135 sq. mi.	St. Christopher (St. Kitts): settled by the British 1623, occupied by the French 1666, restored to Britain 1783. Nevis: settled by the British 1628. Anguilla: settled 1650. Nevis and Anguilla now dependencies of St. Christopher	British colony
ST. LUCIA	99,084	238 sq. mi.	Settled by the French 1660; held alternately by the French and British until 1814, when assigned to Britain	British colony
ST. VINCENT AND NORTHERN GRENADINES	85,000	150 sq. mi.	Disputed by France and Britain until 1783, when St. Vincent became a British possession. The northern Grenadines are now dependencies of St. Vincent	British colony
BRITISH VIRGINS (TORTOLA, VIRGIN GORDA, ANEGADA, JOST VAN DYKES)	8,619	59 sq. mi.	Occupied by Dutch buccaneers until 1648, settled by the British 1666	British colony
ARUBA, BONAIRE, CURAÇAO	198,563	361 sq. mi.	Spanish until 1634, when seized by the Dutch; changed hands several times; Dutch since 1816	Self-governing integral unit of the Netherlands
SABA, SINT EUSTATIUS, SINT MAARTEN	4,956	33 sq. mi.	Saba: first settled by the Dutch 1640, in dispute until permanently assigned to the Dutch in 1814. Sint Maarten: settled by the Dutch and the French (who called their section of the island Saint Martin) in 1648; in dispute until 1814, when France received the northern two thirds of the island, the Netherlands the southern third	Self-governing integral unit of the Netherlands
GUADELOUPE, SAINT BARTHÉLEMY, SAINT MARTIN, DÉSIRADE, MARIE-GALANTE, LES SAINTES	300,000	680 sq. mi.	Guadeloupe: settled by the French 1635, variously held by other powers. Saint Barthélemy, Saint Martin, Désirade, Marie-Galante and Les Saintes are dependencies of Guadeloupe	Overseas *département* of France
MARTINIQUE	310,000	425 sq. mi.	Settled by the French 1635, occupied at different times by the British, French since 1814	Overseas *département* of France

PRINCIPAL CITY	MAJOR SOURCES OF INCOME	RELIGION	LANGUAGE
Havana	Sugar, tobacco, coffee; light industry (sugar processing, textile and cement manufacturing)	Predominantly Roman Catholic	Spanish
Santo Domingo	Sugar, cocoa, coffee, tobacco; limited industry (textiles, cement, glass bottles, paper)	Roman Catholic	Spanish
Port-au-Prince	Coffee, sisal, sugar	Roman Catholic, *Vodou*	French, French Creole
San Juan	Sugar, tobacco, varied light industry, tourism	Predominantly Roman Catholic, some evangelical Protestant sects	Spanish, English
Charlotte Amalie	Sugar, rum, some farming and cattle raising, tourism	Roman Catholic, some Protestant and Jewish communities	English
Kingston	Bauxite and aluminum production, sugar, tourism	Anglican, Roman Catholic	English
Port of Spain, Trinidad	Petroleum production and refining	Roman Catholic, Anglican	English, French Creole
St. John's, Antigua	Sugar and sugar products, tourism	Anglican	English
Nassau, New Providence	Bananas, citrus fruits, cucumbers, fishing, poultry, tourism	Anglican, Roman Catholic, Methodist and other Protestant groups	English
Bridgetown	Sugar and sugar products, tourism	Anglican	English
George Town	Remittances from Cayman seamen who have left the islands, tourism	Presbyterian, Roman Catholic	English
Roseau	Bananas	Roman Catholic, Methodist, Anglican	English, French Creole
St. George's	Nutmeg, cocoa beans, bananas	Anglican, Roman Catholic	English
Plymouth	Cotton, bananas, tomatoes, carrots	Anglican, Roman Catholic	English, French Creole
Basseterre, St. Christopher	Sugar and sugar products, cotton	Anglican, Roman Catholic	English
Castries	Bananas, copra, cocoa, tourism	Roman Catholic	English, French Creole
Kingstown	Bananas, arrowroot	Anglican, Roman Catholic	English
Road Town, Tortola	Livestock raising, tourism	Anglican, Methodist	English
Willemstad, Curaçao	Aruba and Curaçao: oil refining, shipping, tourism. Bonaire: salt production, tourism	Roman Catholic, some Protestant and Jewish communities	Dutch, Papiamento
Philipsburgh, Sint Maarten	Farming, fishing, tourism	Roman Catholic, some Protestant and Jewish communities	English, Dutch
Pointe-à-Pitre	Sugar, bananas, rum, tourism	Predominantly Roman Catholic	French, French Creole
Fort-de-France	Bananas, sugar, rum, tourism	Predominantly Roman Catholic	French, French Creole

Credits

The sources for the illustrations in this book are shown below. Credits for pictures are separated from left to right by commas, top to bottom by dashes.

Cover—Richard Meek
8—Richard Meek
16 through 24—Richard Meek
28, 29—Map by Jean Simpson
31—Richard Meek
32, 33—Leonard McCombe
34 through 37—Richard Meek
41—Culver Pictures
43 through 51—Richard Meek
57—Richard Meek
58, 59—Odette Mennesson-Rigaud, Earl Leaf from Rapho-Guillumette—Odette Mennesson-Rigaud
60—Richard Meek
61—Dan Weiner
62—Richard Meek
70—Dan Weiner
71 through 73—Richard Meek
74—James K. Welsh
75—Flip Schulke from Black Star
76, 77—Richard Meek
78—Map by Bill Dove
83 through 86—Richard Meek
87—Bruce Henderson
88 through 92—Richard Meek
94—Map by Bill Dove
99 through 107—Richard Meek
108, 109—Marc Riboud from Magnum
110—Map by Bill Dove

117—Grey Villet
118, 119—Hank Walker, Lynn Pelham from Rapho-Guillumette, United Press International—Bernard Diederich, Lynn Pelham from Rapho-Guillumette
120—Lynn Pelham from Rapho-Guillumette
121—Michael Rougier—Lynn Pelham from Rapho-Guillumette
122, 123—G. Bohemia, Andrew St. George, Grey Villet
124—Joe Scherschel
125—Henri Cartier-Bresson from Magnum—Patrick Lescat from Black Star
126, 127—Left Lynn Pelham from Rapho-Guillumette; center Pictorial Parade, Don Uhrbrock—Grey Villet; right Henri Cartier-Bresson from Magnum
128, 129—Richard Meek
137—Commonwealth of Puerto Rico
138 through 144—Richard Meek
149—Richard Meek
150, 151—Richard Meek

ACKNOWLEDGMENTS

The editors of this book are indebted to Sidney W. Mintz, Professor, Department of Anthropology, Yale University, and Lambros Comitas, Associate Professor of Anthropology, Columbia University, who read and commented on the text. Valuable assistance was also received from Thomas G. Mathews, Director, the Institute of Caribbean Studies, University of Puerto Rico; Milo Rigaud, author and authority on *vodou;* and Jerome Spar, Professor of Meteorology, New York University. Mr. Harman acknowledges the help and guidance of Harry Hoetink, Research Associate, the Institute of Caribbean Studies; Enid Baa, Librarian, Caribbean Organization, San Juan, Puerto Rico; Ernest A. Carr, author and folklorist, Port of Spain, Trinidad; Earl Parker Hanson, Consultant, the Puerto Rico Department of State; and William A. Trembley, Visiting Lecturer in History, University of the West Indies, Kingston, Jamaica.

Index

This symbol in front of a page number indicates a photograph or painting of the subject mentioned.

xxx

Production staff for Time Incorporated

John L. Hallenbeck (Vice President and Director of Production)

Robert E. Foy, Caroline Ferri and Robert E. Fraser

Text photocomposed under the direction of

Albert J. Dunn and Arthur J. Dunn

Tampa
St. Petersburg
Tampa Bay
Sarasota
FLORIDA
Lake Okeechobee
West End
GRAND BAHAMA
W. Palm Beach
Ft. Lauderdale
Miami
CAPE SABLE
GULF OF MEXICO
Marsh Harbour
GREAT ABACO
B A H A M A
Northeast Providence Channel
ELEUTHERA (Br.)
Governor's Harbour
NEW PROVIDENCE
Nassau
Key West
FLORIDA KEYS
Straits of Florida
ANDROS ISLAND
Arthur's Town
CAT
SAN SALVADOR (WATLING)
GREAT EXUMA
George Town
RUM CAY
LONG
Clarence Town
CROOKED
MAYAGUANA
ACKLINS
Mayaguana Passage
Caicos Pas
I S L A N
25°
YUCATAN
Yucatan Channel
C. CATOCHE
COZUMEL
MEXICO
C. SAN ANTONIO
Pinar del Rio
Artemisa
Guira de Melena
Gulf of Batabanó
ISLE OF PINES
HAVANA
Guanabacoa
Marianao
Matanzas
Güines
Jovellanos
Colón
Cárdenas
Santa Clara
Cruces
Cienfuegos
C U B A
Sagua la Grande
Caibarién
Placetas
Sancti-Spíritus
Ciego de Ávila
Bay of Pi
Trinidad
Tunas de Zaza
Morón
Júcaro
Florida
Gulf of Ana María
Camagüey
Victoria de las Tunas
Nuevitas
Puerto Padre
Gibara
Banes
Holguin
Sagua de Tánamo
Baracoa
CAPE MAISÍ
Matthew Town
LITTLE INAGUA
GREAT INAGUA
G R E A T
Gulf of Guacanayabo
Manzanillo
Bayamo
Palma Soriano
San Luis
Guantánamo
Niquero
SIERRA MAESTRA
C. CRUZ
Santiago de Cuba
Windward Passage
Port-de-Paix
Cap-Haïtien
Fort Libe
Gulf of Gonaïves
Gonaïv
St. Marc
ÎLE DE LA GONÂVE
HAIT
20°
GRAND CAYMAN (Br.)
W
W E S T
E S T
Montego Bay
Savanna-la-Mar
JAMAICA
Spanish Town
May Pen
Kingston
Blue Mt
Blue Mt Peak 7520
Port Antonio
Jamaica Channel
CAPE IROIS
Jérémie
Les Cayes
Léoga
Jacmel
H I S P
A N T
BAY ISLANDS
Trujillo
Tela
La Ceiba
HONDURAS
Coca
Tegucigalpa
MISKITO CAY
C A R I B B E A
15°
NICARAGUA
Matagalpa
Chinandega
León
Lake Managua
Managua
Granada
Lake Nicaragua
Bluefields
OLD PROVIDENCE (Col.)
ST ANDREWS (Col.)
GREAT CORN (Nic.) (Leased to U.S.)
PACIFIC OCEAN
S. Juan
COSTA
Puntarenas
Alajuela
San José
Cartago
Limón
RICA
PAN.
CANAL ZONE (U.S.A.)
Colón
PANAMA
Santa Marta
Barranquilla
Soledad
Ciénaga
Cartagena
COLOMBIA
Marac
Sincelejo
Mompós
PO
10°
Longitude West of Greenwich
85°
80°
75°